PRESSURE PROOFING

How to Increase Personal Effectiveness on the Job and Anywhere Else for That Matter

NYACK COLLEGE MANHATTAN

SAM KLARREICH

D0001392

Routledge
Taylor & Francis Group
New York   London

Routledge
Taylor & Francis Group
270 Madison Avenue
New York, NY 10016

Routledge
Taylor & Francis Group
2 Park Square
Milton Park, Abingdon
Oxon OX14 4RN

Printed in the United States of America on acid-free paper
10 9 8 7 6 5 4 3 2 1

International Standard Book Number-13: 978-0-415-95754-0 (Hardcover)

Library of Congress Cataloging-in-Publication Data

Klarreich, Samuel H.
   Pressure proofing : how to increase personal effectiveness on the job and anywhere else for that matter / Sam Klarreich.
      p. cm.
   Includes bibliographical references and index.
   ISBN 978-0-415-95754-0
   1. Job stress. 2. Stress (Psychology) 3. Stress management. I. Title.

HF5548.85.K56 2007
158.7'2--dc22
                  2007007154

Visit the Taylor & Francis Web site at
http://www.taylorandfrancis.com

and the Routledge Web site at
http://www.routledge.com

Contents

Preface

Do you feel uneasy when you try to relax? Are you overwhelmed by the deadlines you have to meet? Do you get rattled when things don't go your way? Are you impatient with people who work more slowly than you? Do you often get angry? Do you feel things are hopeless? Do you feel like pulling the covers over your head and not getting out of bed?

People are experiencing these reactions at an increasing rate, despite our expanding knowledge about pressure, anxiety, anger, and depression and despite the fact that computers are supposed to make our work lives easier. The effects can be grim. These negative reactions can lead to deteriorating health and a variety of social problems. For an organization, it often means low employee morale and declining productivity.

Over many years as a practicing psychologist, I have counseled individuals from junior ranks to the most senior levels in a variety of businesses and industries. These people had their own

HELPFUL VERSUS DEBILITATING PRESSURE

From now on, set aside the notions of "good pressure" and "bad pressure." It is far too confusing to try to gauge what is good from what is bad. What has been referred to as "good," or "positive" pressure is in essence "arousal." Arousal is the kind of excitement, energy, and enthusiasm that enhances your performance, especially on the job. We all realize that, in order to perform effectively, we must have a certain amount of energy and drive. If we did not have this element of arousal, we would appear lethargic, listless, "not with it"—simply out of touch with things.

What has been referred to as "bad," or "negative," pressure is indeed what we are talking about in this book. It is extreme arousal, arousal that is "over the top." Far from increasing efficiency, it brings about a multitude of harmful consequences for personal health and well-being as well as for on-the-job productivity. Feeling distressed or anxious definitely interferes with your ability to function. For our purposes then, we are focusing on this state of heightened arousal and overstimulation, which is the true culprit and can lead to a serious anxiety problem if not addressed.

Are You a Pressure Magnet?

To determine if you attract pressure, ask yourself these questions:

- Do you get bothered when you have to wait for something?

- Do you find that you do everything, such as eating, talking, and walking, quickly?
- Do you try to do a lot of things at one time?
- Do you have a burning desire to be successful at everything you try?
- Do you find that there is very little time to do all the things that you have to do?
- Are you most comfortable when you are talking about what you are doing rather than what anyone else is doing?
- Does your mind always wander when a person is conversing with you?
- Do you define success as being able to do things faster, but not necessarily better, than your colleagues?
- Do you believe that you and others are judged by performance alone?
- Do you always find yourself competing with and trying to outdo those around you?
- Are you constantly being told by those around you to slow down?

If you answered "yes" to many of these questions, you can probably consider yourself to be a pressure magnet and possibly predisposed to distress and anxiety down the road!

PRESSURE-PRONE PERSONALITIES

Throughout the 1950s and 1960s, a cardiologist named Dr. Meyer Friedman was investigating coronary heart disease. He observed that people with certain personalities and certain behaviors seemed to experience similar health problems. In essence, his research indicated that individuals with certain characteristics were more prone to heart disorders than were individuals without those characteristics. Dr. Friedman subsequently collaborated with another cardiologist, Dr. Ray Rosenman. In their research, they coined the terms "Type A personality" and "Type A behavior." These two individuals drew our attention to the fact that the way people live ultimately influences their health. Some actions can be detrimental to health, perhaps so detrimental that they eventually contribute to heart problems. These early observations contributed greatly, not only to the field of behavioral analysis but also to that of health promotion and health education in the workplace.

As behavior and personality research actively continued into the 1970s and 1980s, it led to a better understanding of the pressure-prone personality. This personality type is in a constant and urgent struggle to accomplish a number of tasks from his or her workplace (or any other place, for that matter) in the least amount of time and, while doing this, challenges anyone who gets in the way. This is the dawn of discovery. We are coming to realize more than ever that the way we live and what we do with our lives, including our working lives, ultimately determines our health and our state of well-being. Furthermore, if we take certain precautions, we may be a lot happier and live longer.

"PRESSURE COOKERS" TODAY

Currently, about 50% to 60% of North Americans may be pressure prone, or at least show some characteristics of being pressure prone. This percentage may appear high; however, when you better understand the behaviors, you begin to realize that many of us have engaged in some of the behaviors that are typical of a "Pressure Cooker" personality.

Pressure Cookers are usually driven to achieve and are very competitive. In the effort to achieve, they come across in an aggressive, impatient manner. It is almost as if they are fighting time. They also seem to be struggling with themselves, with others, and with the world and life in general. They seem to resent the world and people getting in their way. As a result, they appear hostile, angry, and resentful. This hostility and anger can flare up at almost any time.

You might ask yourself: "Who needs this?" and "Who would ever want to work with someone like this?" You'll be happy to know that this behavior is not contagious and that there is some good to being a Pressure Cooker. To begin with, these people strive to achieve a great deal. They push, drive, and attempt to excel at every opportunity. They usually receive recognition for their efforts. A fair amount of social approval usually comes their way from management and supervisors. In addition, they are rewarded for their achievements in a material sense. They may earn more money and, as a result, have bigger homes, drive fancier cars, and wear more expensive clothing than their peers.

In social circles, Pressure Cookers are typically lauded for their achievements. Others often marvel at their ambition and level of accomplishment. Organizations and corporations have, over the years, grown to love Pressure Cookers because they get results. All this seems very good and, in fact, it is good for Pressure Cookers and for their organizations. However, there is a catch: the good news is eventually overwhelmed by bad.

PRESSURE COOKERS CAN OVERHEAT

Ask yourself these questions:

- Do you feel on edge, jumpy, or nervous when faced with tasks that need to be completed?
- Do you find that you are bombarded by and obsessed with the many deadlines that are facing you?
- Do you get rattled easily when things don't go your way?
- Do you get incensed when policies and procedures stand in the way of your progress?
- Do you find that you have no patience or tolerance for others who work more slowly than you do?
- Do you believe that you carry the burden of responsibility for the success of your unit, department, or organization?

- Do you find that you often get angry?
- Do you find that you sometimes speak loudly or swear in order to get your point across?
- Do you find that you regularly pound a table or desk or wave a pencil or ruler in order to draw attention to what you are saying?

If you answered "yes" to many of these questions, you may be a Pressure Cooker about to overheat. Because Pressure Cookers are competitive, they can take competition and other matters just a bit too far. For example, a Pressure Cooker might come up to you and shout, "Let's see who can get into work the earliest and leave the latest." These people constantly struggle to outdo themselves—and others—at every turn.

Pressure Cookers are very involved in numbers. The number of their achievements becomes foremost in their minds. It is almost as if they are concerned about quantity and nothing else. Over time, quality suffers. They believe they are better simply because they do more. Is this really what organizations are looking for?

As Pressure Cookers continue on in their working lives, rushing around, making certain that they accomplish their daily quotas, they get so caught up in numbers that they eventually become liabilities. They make decisions too quickly. They fail to consider long-range plans. They constantly explode at others who obstruct their short-term objectives. They eventually become pains in the neck. Inevitably, they find it difficult to work with others because their colleagues are competitors who may eventually turn into enemies. This type of unhealthy competition is calculated to interfere with Pressure Cookers' work performance. Their solution is to isolate themselves. They find working with others a threat. Since cooperation and teamwork are of utmost importance in business and industry today, how does this type of behavior fit into the picture? It doesn't!

Pressure Cookers also have a tendency to hoard. They do not share their ideas or their work. This can be seriously counterproductive. These people do not delegate or seek support and help. They grab every possible opportunity, collecting them as others might collect toys. Eventually, the work becomes unmanageable. There is simply too much to do and too little time in which to do it. This bad situation gets progressively worse.

I recall working with a manufacturing manager who described what his job was like:

> "It's a bloody rat race in that plant. You can't trust anybody. Some of those characters think they can get my job, but they never will. I can do more work than any two or three of those idiots. I don't share work with anyone. That's how I stay ahead, by working harder and longer. But I'll tell you, it's damn hard doing twenty things at once. I sometimes think I'm going crazy. But it's the only way I can survive in this madhouse!"

Pressure Cookers commonly start to struggle to exert control over an increasingly uncontrollable set of demands. The more uncontrollable things become, the more they try to control them. They find themselves becoming more exhausted and more frustrated, but they push on. They begin to feel a sense of helplessness as the demands mount and the uncontrollable nature of the workload spirals. Because they are so afraid of failing and of not completing tasks, they still push on.

Physical symptoms usually begin to occur. However, Pressure Cookers pretend these symptoms don't exist because they regard them as signs of failure and loss of control. They simply focus on the task at hand, making certain that they complete as much as they can in as little time as possible. Because they do not pay attention to their symptoms, the symptoms usually get worse. If they did pay attention, they would realize that their lifestyle is inappropriate and that their behaviors need to change.

Pressure Cookers become more and more dissatisfied with their work and begin to feel a sense of personal failure. For a Pressure Cooker, this is a fate worse than death. This is also when the bad turns into the ugly. Pressure Cookers' relationships begin to disintegrate. They have more quarrels at home. They spend less time with spouses and children. Friendships are eliminated in favor of increasing hours on the job. Leisure activities are done away with. An appreciation of the simple pleasures in life is exchanged for escalated hours of desperation on the job. They start to treat their spouses and children as if they were subordinates at work. They order them around. They shout at them. They expect them to fall into line. As a result, mutual support and understanding at home is simply abandoned. It gets worse.

At this point, Pressure Cookers walk around with an abundance of hostility. They are easily frustrated and easily provoked to expressions of anger. It is as if they are always ready to do battle with any colleagues they encounter. They rationalize their behaviors. The world, and particularly the workplace, has been so bad to them that they in turn have to be bad to the world and the people they work with. They constantly legitimize their actions and carry on in an obnoxious fashion. They may also begin to consume more alcohol, smoke more cigarettes, and generally abuse their health. They sleep less, they eat more irregularly, and they isolate themselves from key support people around them.

Is it any wonder that anger, abuse, and even violence at the workplace and at home have escalated? Road rage, desk rage, computer rage, harassment, spousal abuse, child abuse, elder abuse, and even pet abuse rates have burgeoned!

An advertising executive explained his rut this way:

> It got so bad that I hated myself and everyone around me. I hated my body because it let me down. I was getting dizzy, sweaty, short of breath. I was experiencing headaches, chest pains, stomachaches. But darn it, I figured that I would just work harder and it would go away. It never did.
>
> And those fools I worked with, I hated them as well. They got in the way of everything. They always told me that I looked bad, that I should slow down. What the heck did they know? They didn't know the pressure I was under. My family wasn't any better. They always wanted me to come home and spend more time with them. How the heck was I supposed to do that when I was always faced with at least half a dozen deadlines? The only safe hiding place was in my office, where I could be alone.

After a time, Pressure Cookers become Jekyll and Hydes, growing unpredictable, moody, and suffering from personality shifts. One day they may be very angry; the next, very depressed; and a day or two later, very up and excited. When Pressure Cookers are angry, they are angry at the world, the company, their family, and their friends. When they are depressed, they are pessimistic, cynical, overburdened, and overwhelmed. They are guilt-ridden. They blame themselves for every mess they have gotten into and the messes everyone else has gotten into. They believe that they will never get out of their rut. On the other hand, when they are up, they can conquer the world. They can achieve it all. They can regain their success and accomplish what they always wanted to accomplish.

This does not happen to all Pressure Cookers. But those who have a tendency to overheat usually end up in such a predicament. Without question, we all engage in unhealthy behaviors in certain situations; however, most of us do not engage in those behaviors throughout all of the situations that we experience from day to day. If you find yourself engaging in Pressure Cooker behaviors to the point of overheating frequently and regularly, you have reason to be concerned about the quality of your life.

Pressure Cookers Can Crack

Overheating behavior inflicts a lot of punishment on the body, with many resulting physical complications. Pressure Cookers who overheat usually exercise less, smoke more cigarettes, eat meals that are high in cholesterol and animal fat, and have more serum cholesterol and serum fat in the blood. These lifestyle actions can pose a health problem, but are only part of the problem for Pressure Cookers. When these behaviors are combined with certain other characteristics, overheated Pressure Cookers face a serious risk for coronary heart disease.

As Pressure Cookers do their thing in their own crazy fashion, whether at work or elsewhere, specific physical changes affect them. Because they are always running around anxious and angry, as if they are chasing time, their bodies react by releasing adrenaline and a stress hormone called *cortisol* into the bloodstream. Heart rate, blood pressure, and stomach acid production all increase. Once adrenaline rises in the bloodstream, it has been known to cause lesions or small tears in the inner lining of the arteries, particularly the coronary arteries. If these arteries are weak to begin with, the lesions may ultimately cause severe heart problems.

The complications do not stop there. Adrenaline and cortisol have also been known to contribute to the formation of blood platelets. These platelets accumulate in the arteries and have been linked to arteriosclerosis, or "hardening of the arteries," which also contributes to heart disease. As Pressure Cookers continue to act in harmful ways, the steady flow of adrenaline works away at the arteries, causing damage that might ultimately damage the heart.

A marketing representative who came to me for help recalled a terrifying experience:

> I was always running in ten different directions, sometimes wondering what I was trying to accomplish. Anyone who got in my way really got a blast from me, boy! In fact, I fought with a lot of people I worked with, because they weren't on the ball and often made me look bad. While I was running around chasing time and quarreling with people, I just didn't feel right. I sometimes felt like I was going to pass out. One day, I had a heart attack at work! The ambulance came and they carried me out on a stretcher. That experience changed my life!

Intense anger and hostility seem to be very important components of Pressure Cooker behavior. They have been linked to coronary heart disease and high blood pressure. Picture this angry, hostile person running around, talking quickly, exploding all over the place, shouting, and throwing fits. It is not hard to see why all of a sudden he would have an increase in heart rate and an accompanying increase in blood pressure. This person would also probably begin to produce adrenaline, which could lead to permanent heart damage. Each and every time the Pressure Cooker gets wound up, agitated, disturbed, suspicious, and totally wrapped up in this anger and hostility, he may be putting his health at risk.

That is not to say that we should never get angry. We all get angry once in a while, but we usually get rid of the anger fairly quickly. However, intransigent Pressure Cookers seem to experience very intense anger for long periods of time. In a sense, they are driving themselves into the ground. By regularly increasing their heart rates, blood pressure, and adrenaline production in the bloodstream, they are repeatedly forcing their bodies into unnecessary overdrive. How much of this can their bodies take?

The other significant component, aside from hostility, is the behavior called "time urgency," also labeled "hurry disease." This is the anxious side of our Pressure Cooker, who is chronically impatient, worrying about doing things too slowly, chasing time. The Pressure Cooker is obsessed with speed and frenetically tries to do more and more over a shorter period of time. He or she experiences much the same bodily reaction associated with anger and hostility. Again, the heart rate goes up, blood pressure rises, and probably those same stress hormones or adrenaline enter the bloodstream, presenting a serious risk to health. Whether the task is difficult or easy, Pressure Cookers still run around as if they have had their heads cut off.

You can begin to appreciate how anger and time urgency can affect your health in general, and your heart in particular. Furthermore, I hope you now recognize why overheated Pressure Cooker behavior is regarded as a serious health risk. Pressure Cookers overmobilize their bodies. Whether they need to go into high gear or not, they have trained themselves to be frenzy machines.

To Self-Destruct or Not to Self-Destruct?

Not all Pressure Cookers are on a course of self-destruction. Some have really excessive workloads, some have standards that are too high, and some are threatened too easily. These people may be unable to cope with the pressures and chaos around them. But these scenarios are minor compared to the problems created by the two toxic demons of Pressure Cooker behavior. Pressure Cookers who indulge in time urgency and anger and hostility are truly unhealthy and can be regarded as time bombs ready to go off.

Let me comment on a myth that currently pervades our society about people who work excessively, commonly labeled as "workaholics." Over the years, workaholics have also been regarded as "time bombs." In fact, it is almost considered a sin to be a workaholic. But many workaholics lead very happy and successful lives and are also very healthy. Workaholism is not deleterious to well-being. People who enjoy their work and are excited about it, who jump out of bed every morning looking forward to more, are generally very contented people. They also enjoy relationships with others, often in the same enthusiastic manner with which they engage in work. This makes for a very invigorating way of life. These people are stimulating to be around. Yet we devalue these people; we think that they are crazy. In fact, we probably envy their enthusiasm and energy.

A lawyer described her work schedule to me:

> You know, I put in seventy to eighty hours of work each week—and I love it. I thoroughly enjoy what I do and the people I work with. I never get a cold or a sore throat, and I never miss work. When I went to visit my family doctor, she said I was as healthy as a horse. I feel great, enthusiastic, and energetic. I have plenty of reserve energy for my family and my friends. And yes, they are very important parts of my life. I do run into occasional disagreements with my

husband and kids about not being available for certain functions, but we usually iron out our differences and, as a result, we understand ourselves better.

However, if workaholics, or healthy Pressure Cookers, were to engage in a constant expression of anger and time urgency, they would begin to experience the same symptoms and problems that we talked about earlier. This is when a happy workaholic turns into an unhappy, distressed, and ultimately burned-out individual or an unhealthy Pressure Cooker who is apt to self-destruct.

Personality Type Versus Behavior

Certain individuals typically have been described as having no driving urge, no desire to succeed. They do not have a strong need to accomplish. They can relax without feeling guilty. They seem to engage in activities with others for the enjoyment and pleasure of the experience, not necessarily to compete, to dominate, or to drive the opposition into the ground. They seem to know what their limitations are and are able to accept them. They strive for what they want, but they go after it without frenzy or hurry.

In addition, they are not overly sensitive to other people's reactions. If they receive criticism, they usually take it reasonably well. They seem to be intelligent and ambitious in that they take time to contemplate the future. They can examine short-term goals and think about long-term opportunities as well. They don't seem to be driven by the need to get immediate results. According to cardiologists Friedman and Rosenman, these personalities can be classified as "Type B personalities," different from Pressure Cookers and the previously described Type A personalities.

Is a Type A personality, or Pressure Cooker, at one extreme and a Type B personality at the other extreme? What exists between Type A and Type B? In answer to these queries, Friedman and Rosenman developed five personality categories.

- The first category is the fully developed Type A, or the Pressure Cooker.
- The second type is a moderately developed Type A.
- The third type is the moderately developed Type B.
- The fourth type is the fully developed Type B.
- Finally, the fifth type is a mixture of Type A and Type B behaviors.

Complicated? Yes, it is. Are there truly such distinct types? No, I don't believe so. Most of us are probably in the fifth category. We sometimes do things that can be classified as Pressure Cooker or Type A behaviors, and we sometimes do things that can be classed as Type B acts. We don't have to concern ourselves with the appropriate label. What is most important is what we do in certain situations. If we do things that are harmful to us in particular situations (especially indulging in the most harmful behaviors—time urgency and anger and hostility), then we ought to try to correct that.

Hardships and Hassles

"Hardships and hassles" are basically events, situations, or changes that take place in our work lives or personal lives. A great deal has been written about the variety of changes that can produce pressure. Many of us have been convinced that the more change we experience, the more pressured we will be. Some individuals have become so worried that they begin to think, "My gosh, I'd better not experience any more changes; otherwise I'll be anxious to the point where I'll crack up." Perhaps few of us go so far, but it is critical to realize that pressure is not simply caused by change.

However, some people have invested a lot of energy and time in listing all sorts of events that they regard as anxiety producers. Severe situations, or hardships, include

- Termination from a job
- Terminal illness
- Death of a colleague or associate
- A demotion
- A new job
- A decrease in income
- Conflict with a colleague or supervisor
- Overqualification or underqualification for one's job
- Interaction with people who are aggressive
- Restructuring, reorganizing, or downsizing
- Death of a spouse or family member

- Separation, divorce, or marriage
- Shock or trauma of a natural disaster
- House break-in
- Sale or purchase of a house

Many other events are described as *hassles,* which are less severe than hardships and occur more frequently in our everyday lives. These include

- Difficulties with in-laws
- Relocation to a new neighborhood
- Vacation
- Holidays
- Competition with a colleague
- Transfer to a new position or department
- Noisy environment
- Uncommunicative colleagues or supervisors
- Car problems
- Traffic jams
- Lateness for appointments

If we were to believe that all of the above life changes cause tension, then we would virtually have to stop living to avoid pressure. Changes are important, but they do not necessarily cause problems. If they did, then everyone who experienced these changes would experience the same degree of discomfort.

Consider divorce, which has often been referred to as a major hardship. We know that four or five of every ten marriages end in divorce. It would seem to follow that sooner or later a lot of people would become extremely disturbed and have their lives greatly disrupted. But this is not the case. Some people are delighted to be divorced and view divorce as a positive change, a step forward. In fact, a local college even offered a course entitled "Creative Divorce." The originator of the program took the view that divorce is the first step to a new and enriched life.

The president of a union spoke to me about his divorce:

> I thought I would be completely shattered but, to my surprise, I wasn't. I realized that my wife and I were both unhappy and we simply weren't able to live together anymore. You know, we actually get along better now that we are divorced. In fact, we go out together once in a while and we truly enjoy each other's company. Divorce has been a godsend for both of us.

Being fired is a critical hardship for a lot of people. Here again, we assume that anyone who is fired experiences tremendous anxiety and discomfort. But this is not necessarily so. Some people are almost delighted to be dismissed. This is not to say that we should all go out of our way to get fired. It simply means that some people view this hardship differently. They think things through and come to the conclusion that they are going to receive a good severance arrangement; they have an opportunity to explore exciting new options; they are leaving an environment that is too uncompromising; they will be able to work with different, maybe more exciting, individuals; they will have new opportunities for advancement; and they will simply be happier now that they are no longer a member of a team that they never really felt part of.

I remember talking to an administrator who, in the course of a year, left one job and started another, sold his house and bought another, and went through a divorce. In addition, an important member of his family passed away and his daughter suffered a serious illness. You might suppose that this man must have gone crazy because of the pressure he experienced. In fact, he indicated that he was never healthier than he was during this period. There was so much going on and he was spending so much energy in managing all these changes that he felt more vibrant than he ever had before.

Let me give you another example: a death, especially the death of a spouse. I think we would all agree that this would be a major event in our lives. Many people would state categorically that this event inevitably brings on anxiety, but this is not necessarily true. Some people have found that the burial of their spouse was a chance for them to begin to live again. They view it almost as an inspiration. One man told me: "My wife was in pain. Thank God she has passed away." Another client said: "I was going through tremendous pain while my husband was suffering. Now I feel such relief. I know he has now passed on to a more serene and beautiful place." How you perceive an apparently troubling event is the critical factor. In some cultures, death is viewed as another step toward a life hereafter. Death is seen as a wonderful experience, a transition to the other side. In these cultures, distress would be the last reaction to death.

Let us look at robbery as a hardship. I think that we would all agree that being the victim of a robbery is a very critical experience. Again, we might assume that anyone who has gone through it would be extremely upset for a long time. However, this is not accurate; robbery is not harmful in the same way for all victims. Some victims seem to suffer the symptoms of anxiety more than others because of the way they perceive the event. Some victims view the robbery experience as devastating and say to themselves: "I cannot stand this anymore. I hate people. I am never going to be able to survive this. My home is ruined forever. I will never feel comfortable in this house again. I am going to be depressed for the rest of my life. I hate everybody because of how destructive they are. There is no way that I can ever sleep here for fear that it will happen again." If you were to view robbery in this fashion, you would have no choice but to be distressed. That is not to say that robbery, as an event, is not upsetting; it is. But you do not necessarily have to be severely and chronically disturbed by it. Victims who apparently are less distressed and disturbed view robbery in a different way. They say to themselves: "This is not the end of the world. If I'm lucky, this will never happen to me again. My home was burglarized but not destroyed. Items were stolen but most can be replaced. Those important possessions that can't be replaced, I will cherish in my memory." It is these views that are important. This perspective tends to minimize pressure, no matter what hardship occurs.

A very significant hardship is trauma. Let us take the example of a major disaster, say a hurricane or a tornado that has just wiped out a community. Most people would assume that if your home and everything inside it are destroyed, you would be devastated and physically and psychologically ruined. But people do not always react in the same way and, thus, do not experience the same degree of pressure. Indeed, some people seem to cope better with disaster. Their perceptions make the difference. A person who is likely to be extremely disturbed and bothered might think: "I will never get over this. I will never be able to go on. God was rotten to me." Others might think: "The world is evil and everyone in it is evil. Why did this have to happen to me and my family? I will never be able to get back on my feet. I am going to be miserable for the rest of my life. How will I ever continue? I am ruined."

Those who perceive things differently have a significantly reduced level of disturbance to endure. I do not intend to deprecate the importance of a traumatic event or hardship. What I am emphasizing is the importance of your outlook. Individuals whose distress is minimized might think, "The fact that my home is ruined does not mean that my life is ruined. I have my health, my family members have their health, and we can go on. If I built it up once, I can build it up again. Not only can I survive, but I am looking forward to the challenge; a challenge like this will bring our family together. If we can survive this, we can survive anything. I lost my loved one, my soul mate, and I will grieve and be saddened for the rest of my life, but I will not let myself be destroyed. I know that my soul mate would want me to carry on."

We need not be controlled by the changes in our lives. The fact that we encounter hardships and hassles does not mean that we are destined to suffer. Many of us have been brainwashed to believe that we are victims, slaves of our environment. Those who are convinced that they are victims go around dramatizing, "catastrophizing," talking doom and gloom. Their perspectives are warped.

It may appear that I am recommending positive thinking: "Just follow the message of this book and everything will be wonderful! Think positively and our problems will be solved!" In fact, I am not necessarily endorsing positive thinking, but I am recommending the adoption of a realistic view. A perspective that is based on what you are faced with, here and now, is the starting point. A sensible, logical, even optimistic outlook can turn things around. If you have the choice to either experience or avoid pressure, which would you choose? Of course, you would choose not to experience these symptoms. And the choice *is* yours! You can maximize or minimize your unhealthy reactions by paying attention to your outlook. It is your thinking that makes an event problematic.

Remember this: You are entitled to feel concern, you are entitled to feel upset, and you are entitled to mourn and grieve for your losses. These reactions are human and natural. Such normal reactions do not, however, have to result in chronic or severe pressure and anxiety that is debilitating and health destroying.

Sick Organization Syndrome

We have all become very sensitive to events within organizations. We often believe that situations in the work environment produce our problems. I do not rule out the importance of organizational factors. However, I believe that we can largely determine what will be problematic, and how much it will interfere with our lives, by the views we uphold, irrespective of what goes on in the workplace. Some specialists in human resources, organizational development, and organizational effectiveness might take issue with this. But it seems to me that if conditions within an organization caused all pressure, then everyone in that environment would suffer to the same degree, at the same time. This just does not happen. Certain people think one way and experience difficulties, whereas other people think another way and undergo minimal discomfort. To say that the company is "doing us in" is incorrect. We do ourselves in. There may be certain work conditions that require change, but this is a separate issue. In order to reduce distress, people must first examine what is going on inside their heads. Then they can take a look at their work environments and decide what changes to go for.

A data processing manager discussed his philosophy with me:

I always blamed the company for my problems. Because I had so many meetings to attend, so many deadlines to meet, so many outdated policies to contend with, so many hassles from my client groups to handle, I was always nervous, tense, and irritable. If only the company would be more sensitive to my needs and make my life a little bit easier, I was sure I'd feel a lot better. But one day I looked around at other managers. Some of them seemed to be handling matters quite well. They had the same hassles I did; yet, they weren't as uptight. After talking to them, I found out that their thinking was different. They didn't take things so seriously and, therefore, the everyday problems didn't get to them as much. Then I realized that maybe I was the problem. Perhaps I was just too worried about too many things. That's not to say that my company is perfect! But maybe I was too demanding both of myself and of those around me. I'll tell you, once I stopped driving myself crazy, I got more work done. Also, I was able to change some of the things which bugged me, because people finally listened to me and stopped seeing me as a royal pain in the behind.

The Meaning of Pressure

Pressure and most anxiety constitute a physiological and psychological response to events that are perceived as threats to one's well-being. In simple terms, pressure consists of a variety of symptoms that result from an incident or a situation that you see as a threat. It may involve a colleague, supervisor, workload, family, friend, or neighbor. Because you hold this view, the incident is typically managed very poorly and ineffectively. The key element is what you as an individual regard as a threat to your health and well-being.

2 Unhealthy Thinking Leads to Unhealthy Consequences

There is nothing either good or bad, but thinking makes it so.

William Shakespeare

Whether we realize it or not, we are all thinkers. In fact, it would be safe to say that we are chronic thinkers. Each and every day we ponder something or other. We think in many different ways. Sometimes we talk to ourselves and reflect in words, phrases, and sentences. Other times we visualize certain images and think to ourselves in pictures, fantasies, and dreams. Often, after we have thought about what has happened at work or at home, we rehearse what we should have done or said and how we should have felt.

As humans, we have a tendency to think rationally, realistically, and reasonably. However, we also have a propensity to think irrationally, unrealistically, and unreasonably, and when we do, we are likely to experience a variety of harmful feelings and symptoms. These problematic feelings include anxiety, worry, fear, anger, and depression. On the other hand, if we choose to think rationally, reasonably, and realistically, we are more likely to experience helpful, comfortable feelings that are not problematic—such as concern, compassion, sorrow, love, joy, happiness, and contentment.

We have a choice. We can choose to think in nonsensical terms or in sensible terms. That choice largely determines how we feel. If we feel pressured, we can assume that our heads are filled with unsound, absurd, unhealthy nonsense!

To further confuse matters, we sometimes think about the way in which we think. If we think irrationally and unreasonably and bring on distress, we begin to worry about the crazy ideas that are running through our heads. We then upset ourselves further and create even more pressure by thinking we are crazy because of the way we are thinking. Complicated, yes!

Act Before You Think?

Our society is very big on doing, not thinking. In almost every major organization and corporation, the emphasis is on problem solving, completing tasks, getting the job done. Action is seen as the first and foremost activity. Thinking is secondary.

Dr. Edward De Bono (1984), who created the concept of "lateral thinking," has pointed out that "our conceptual area is the critical area." He believes that "the quality of our future is going to be designed by the quality of our thinking." Organizations and industries around the world would benefit tremendously if they encouraged more thinking. Problem solving should be secondary to thinking.

Under the circumstances, it is not surprising that many employees struggle with pressure. They are encouraged to solve the problem quickly and get it out of the way: "If you have a problem with pressure, do something about it! Get your life in order and get on with it!" But how can people be expected to get on with managing their lives unless they think about it first?

FIGHT OR FLIGHT

When we were cavemen and cavewomen, we frequently must have found ourselves in positions where we needed to fight in order to preserve our lives. We could be attacked at any time by all sorts of interesting and frightening creatures. We always had to be ready for combat. Our bodies prepared us by releasing certain hormones into the bloodstream. Adrenaline caused the heart to react. The muscles would then respond, and the brain would be prepared. Our bodies were primed for battle. When we were scared and chose not to do battle, we would run. The body would prepare itself in the same way. The brain, the heart, the stomach, and the muscles were all ready for running.

Today, we often react to problems as we used to when we were cavemen and cavewomen. We act as if our very lives are being threatened. We fight or run! This reaction makes sense if we are being attacked by animals that could kill us. But in the workplace, wild animals are not likely to threaten us, although some coworkers may appear to act like animals. Yet certain people seem to think such a threat exists. They view their colleagues as beasts and their supervisors and managers as creatures from some black lagoon! Furthermore, they react physically to the perception, as if the threats were real, by preparing themselves to fight or flee. These people repeatedly put extraordinary pressure on themselves and their bodies. Their faulty perceptions of situations make them become victims of distress.

Sixteen Hazardous Thoughts

Unhealthy, unreasonable thinking manufactures pressure. Normal events in the workplace and outside are transformed by our thinking into threatening situations that become hazardous to our well-being.

Two main categories of events give us grief. One group relates to tasks, projects, and assignments—in general, to work. The other group relates to colleagues and managers—in general, to people. Our thinking about these events involves a great deal of worrying, agonizing, and "catastrophizing." People are plagued with dread about some possible disaster that may be waiting for them around the corner. What follows is a variety of panic-laden thoughts revolving around events in the workplace—thoughts that get us into trouble.

1. SOMETHING TERRIBLE WILL HAPPEN TO ME IF I MAKE A MISTAKE.

In this case, the person is terrified of making an error. He is convinced that he is going to be criticized by his manager. He worries that he may be fired. He dwells on the terrible things that are bound to happen if he makes a mistake. Is this reasonable? Is it realistic? Of course not! But many people spend a lot of time worrying about doing something incorrectly. They become so fearful that at times they stop performing altogether or actually make more errors than they ordinarily would.

2. THERE IS A RIGHT WAY AND A WRONG WAY TO DO THINGS.

It is obviously right to succeed and be a sensation on the job. It is equally obviously wrong to fail, because something awful will happen. Work is usually not a simple matter of success or failure, but hordes of people have this black-and-white view of the work world. They constantly feel threatened when things aren't correct, whatever "correct" really means. If something were truly "right," then we would all be doing the "right" thing. However, certain people behave as if there exists a true right and drive themselves crazy trying to achieve it.

3. IT IS AWFUL AND HORRIBLE TO BE CRITICIZED.

The person who thinks this is convinced that if she is criticized she must be a failure in the eyes of management, colleagues, and friends. What's more, all these people must think that she is incompetent. Once she has been put down, she will never be able to recover. Some people constantly fear severe reactions from others. Criticism is a common feature of the working day and life in general, and sometimes it may be destructive rather than constructive. But it is not reasonable to fear all criticism.

4. I MUST RECEIVE APPROVAL ALL THE TIME.

Certain people have a strong need for positive feedback. They pray that management or family will tell them that they are doing a great job, because then they can feel like winners and walk with their heads held high for everyone to see.

All of us would like to receive positive feedback and commendation, but is it so awful if we don't get it? Yet certain employees feel that they can't go on without their regular dose.

5. I MUST BE COMPETENT AND MUST BE VIEWED THAT WAY.

This type of person demands that management rate him extremely highly and that his colleagues tell him that his performance is extraordinary. What if this does not occur? Does it mean that the person has failed? Does it mean that he will never amount to anything in the organization? Some people really believe that this is the case and worry about it.

6. PEOPLE IN AUTHORITY SHOULD NEVER BE CHALLENGED.

In other words, if I disagree with my supervisor, I will probably be fired. Or, if I have a debate with a colleague, he will think I am a terrible person to work with and have nothing to do with me. Certain people take on a multitude of jobs, even if they are overworked, simply because they are afraid to say "no." They feel that saying no might cause disagreement, which means they might not receive approval, might be viewed as incompetent, and might be identified as troublemakers. Surely this is a bit far-fetched! No employee can hope to cooperate fully with everyone 100% of the time. He or she sometimes has to challenge what supervisors and colleagues say and do.

There has been some intriguing research in the area of cooperative relationships, particularly friendships. It appears that the most trusted friends are those who agree with us sometimes but disagree with us at other times. In other words, we appreciate honesty in thought and expression of feeling more than we appreciate mere passive agreement. However, when there is constant agreement or constant disagreement, there is friction. If you constantly disagree, obviously you are going to have trouble forming any kind of relationship, let alone friendships. On the other hand, if you constantly go out of your way to say, "Yes, I agree," other people will not trust your judgment or fully accept your friendship.

Now, apply this principle to the workplace: If you are a typical person who always says, "Yes, I will do this or that," what happens? Some colleagues and managers are simply not going to trust you. Clearly, it is not in your best interest to be constantly agreeable. At times you should disagree, not for the sake of disagreeing, but to voice your opinion and thought. Your working relationships will be more meaningful as a result.

7. LIFE IN THE WORKPLACE MUST BE FAIR AND JUST.

What does "fair and just" really mean? For certain individuals, it means that management should listen to what they say—and furthermore, colleagues should agree with what they say. After all, they are the experts; they know what they are doing. How realistic are thoughts like these? How reasonable is it to believe that I should be treated differently than others? Well, certain people believe that if they are not treated in this fashion, they will be unable to tolerate it. If they don't receive justice by their reckoning, they will feel insecure, ill at ease, and threatened. It becomes very difficult for them to get any work done, let alone maintain relationships at work or outside.

8. I MUST BE IN CONTROL AT ALL TIMES, OTHERWISE I'LL AMOUNT TO NOTHING.

Otherwise I'll amount to nothing. The person who believes this has to be continually bright and alert. He thinks that he must respond brilliantly, especially in the presence of management, to every situation that arises. He feels that once he comes across in this magnificent fashion, he will acquire all the positive feedback he desires and will always be viewed as competent and capable.

If he doesn't receive this feedback, who knows what terrible things will happen to him? Is it possible to be bright and alert all the time? Of course not. Yet certain people feel that this is their mandate in life. How else will they shine and achieve their goals? Their peers and supervisors must regard them as supreme beings. Clearly, this is another line of thinking that can get you into trouble and generate a lot of panic!

9. I MUST ANTICIPATE EVERYTHING, OTHERWISE I'LL NEVER GET AHEAD.

This idea contains others, such as: "I must know what is going on in my manager's head" and "I must be prepared to handle everything and anything that my colleagues dish out." Certain individuals pride themselves on being able to read everybody's vibrations. They would like to think that they have the power to second-guess people, that they can always stay one step ahead of them. Then, and only then, will they be able to win in their competition for success and glory.

I'm a psychologist. I'm supposed to be able to read people's thoughts, but I'm not very good at it. However, certain people are convinced that they can read vibrations and more or less predict what people will say and do. This makes no sense, but try to persuade them that it doesn't! Furthermore, once they guess incorrectly, just try to convince them that their judgment is faulty, especially if they believe their careers are on the line. You'll have a full-blown battle on your hands! And when they finally recognize that their reasoning is faulty, that it was only guesswork and that they are as human as anyone else, what a shock! Anxiety, worry, and fear soon follow.

10. I MUST HAVE THINGS THE WAY I WANT THEM.

If I don't, that proves to the world that I haven't made it. This really means: "I must have a prestigious position, a beautiful office, and a fantastic salary." Certain people are convinced that this line of thinking makes sense. When the things they want do not materialize, they believe that they have somehow failed themselves and those around them. Many become angry when they don't get what they feel they deserve. After all, they have pushed and striven for success.

Again, if you think this way, you are setting yourself up for tremendous disillusionment and possible anxiety by subscribing to these unreasonable thoughts. Yet certain people do not think that their ideas are unrealistic. Thus, when their demands are not fulfilled, their worlds cave in.

11. PEOPLE WHO ARE WRONG SHOULD BE PUNISHED.

If they are not, the organization will surely collapse. Some people are intolerant of others around them, especially colleagues who make mistakes. At the same time, they are worried that the company will go under if justice isn't meted out. These people may think that a person who makes a mistake should be demoted. Of course, those who are intolerant, being outstanding employees, should be promoted in the other's place. Furthermore, they think that if management does not promote them and does not demote the incompetent person with whom they work, then the manager should be taken to task. This attitude may seem extraordinary, but there are those who place themselves above everybody else and are angry when others are not doing things the way they should. They really believe that others who don't live up to their high standards should be punished. They pride themselves on their ability to determine who should be admonished and who should not.

No wonder these people have difficulty getting along with their colleagues! They are convinced that they know everything, including right from wrong. If others do not measure up, then they should be doomed to failure.

Isn't this grossly unrealistic? If you stroll around your department with these thoughts in mind, you are setting yourself up for trouble. You are bound to become alienated from your colleagues. Your job performance will be adversely affected. Ultimately, you are putting yourself under unbearable pressure and will suffer at least some symptoms of stress and anger.

A senior stockbroker talked to me about a problem he had:

> I always walked around as if I had a chip on my shoulder. I knew everything. I couldn't be bothered talking to the people I worked with, because they were a waste of time. After a while, I began to realize that I didn't have anyone to talk to. I had become so used to avoiding people that now people were avoiding me. I started to get down on myself and I noticed that my work started to slip. It's hard coming in to work everyday and being totally alone and isolated. But I guess I created this mess.

12. I MUST HAVE SOMEBODY'S SHOULDER TO CRY ON.

The person who believes this feels that he can't get out of a problem without the total support of others. He also needs to have management feel sorry for him. Typically, when this individual gets into a tough spot, he expects the world to react immediately. He expects his working group to comfort, reassure, and sympathize with him. He is terrified that the pressure will be too much and that he will cave in. To prevent a collapse, he must be bolstered by people around him. If he obtains the support he craves, then he feels that he can make it after all. This reasoning is pretty far-fetched. Certainly, having people nurture you when you feel down is nice. But what if they don't? What if you do not receive the understanding and consideration that you demand? There is no reason to believe that you are going to come apart at the seams, although the conviction may become a self-fulfilling prophecy.

13. I MUST FEEL PERFECT ALL THE TIME, OTHERWISE I'LL NEVER SUCCEED.

Feeling perfect, when you think about it, is a complicated notion. Certain people believe that they must not feel nervous or anxious or get discouraged or down. They think that everybody should be up, everybody should be with it, everybody should be smiling and completely happy. Successful people never get discouraged, or down, or nervous, or jumpy. People who experience any of these negative feelings have failed.

Talk about a heavy load to carry! Everyone feels uncomfortable at times; everyone feels down. It's normal and human to experience a wide variety of feelings. Our emotions may range from ecstasy and joy to feelings of discouragement, discomfort, and nervousness. No one can feel perfect all the time.

14. MY WORTH AS A PERSON IS EXACTLY CORRELATED WITH MY PERFORMANCE.

I'd better perform extraordinarily well; otherwise who can tell what unfortunate fate will befall me? This thought is critical. It is a common premise that pervades the minds of many people walking the corporate corridors.

Countless people mistakenly believe that who they are is determined by what they do inside and outside the workplace. If they perform well on the job, they will probably think that they are wonderful human beings, tremendous performers, and assets to the firm. Should they not execute their jobs well, however, they will persuade themselves that they are no good, incompetent, worthless, and outright failures. No wonder their feelings go up and down like a yo-yo!

These individuals are bound to think that they, and anyone else, must be real idiots to blow a project or a particular job. Of course, they aren't. If they don't do well at something, it simply means that they haven't done well! There is no reason for those people to condemn themselves.

Certain people tend to generalize. They think that because they failed on the job, they will perform inadequately everywhere. In other words, if they have been lousy employees, they will be lousy parents and contemptible spouses. They will conduct themselves amateurishly in the social arena. They will be careless listeners, miserable friends, and social misfits. What's more, they will be inferior lovers. Because they did not meet their own high standards on the job, they expect never to do anything well again. Of course, this line of reasoning is ridiculous! But this is the way certain people think and thus consign themselves to a private purgatory.

15. I WAS PROMISED A CORPORATE ROSE GARDEN.

This thought implies that work activities must always be rewarding and satisfying. As these individuals continue to carry out their responsibilities, management must be considerate toward them and show them respect. If they don't receive what's coming to them, they won't stand for it. After all, why would they go to work unless it was completely gratifying and everyone treated them with courtesy and admiration? Again, I submit that this line of thought does not make sense.

There are, however, a number of people who parade around the workplace thoroughly convinced that this is the way things should be, and if they are not, watch out! It is almost as if there are well-formulated rules carved in stone about the way working conditions should be arranged and the way people should behave. It would be great if one's job was completely rewarding and satisfying, if our opinions were valued and even acted on. But that does not happen very often.

16. It is too late for me to change, and if you expect it, I won't be able to handle it.

People who think this way make it very clear that they are determined to stay the way they are. They are unable to make any meaningful modifications because they read somewhere that people are no longer capable of change after the age of 21.

Characters like this do exist. They make it quite clear to their managers, colleagues, and family that they plan to behave in a rigid, uncompromising fashion and that people around them will have to accept this. Furthermore, they have persuaded themselves that their ill-conceived actions are part of their personalities and can never be altered. They are convinced that, because their behavior contributed to their success in the past, it must be upheld now, even though they may be having problems with work, with management, and with colleagues and friends. In addition, they are afraid to change because they might fail if they try something new. These people are unbending in their determination to remain the same. When they receive an unsatisfactory performance review, they are likely to quit, saying that management is crazy. They will not accept that what they are doing is inappropriate. At most, they may concede that their methods have not been applied with enough thoroughness or enthusiasm.

They are certain that sooner or later their old formula will regain for them the success that they desperately crave. There are lots of these characters around—and they repeatedly get themselves into trouble because of their pigheaded, panic-ridden thinking.

I recall speaking to a financial analyst who really hurt her career with her stubborn approach:

> I always believed that I was right and that I never had to change. Because I experienced success early in my career, I thought that I had the magic formula for success—my way or nothing. I knew that I was bright. I scored at the top every year at university and I was voted by my graduating class as the one most likely to succeed. When I first joined the company, I impressed everyone immediately. I was pegged as a "fast-tracker," a "water-walker." I had all the right stuff. My decisions were impeccable.
>
> But when I moved into the ranks of management, my problems started. I didn't seem to be able to manage people well. I only expected from them what I expected from myself–nothing less than perfection. I was repeatedly warned about my demanding, authoritarian approach. Many times, I was asked to change my management style. However, I was convinced that it was my staff's fault. If they would only do what I told them, everything would be fine. And what the heck did my own manager know? She had been with the company too long, and her ideas were outdated. She didn't have half the talent or brainpower I had. So I stuck to my guns because I knew that I was right and also because I was fearful to find out that I might be wrong. Until, one fateful afternoon, I was asked to leave the company.

Paying the Consequences

DUMB AND DUMBER

We have spent considerable time talking about some of the unhealthy thinking that we can engage in. We now know that if the thinking is worrisome enough, it sets the stage for a lot of bodily reactions, which we label as "pressure." Unhealthy thinking not only leads to uncomfortable feelings but it also prepares us for some dumb actions—actions that do not achieve any meaningful results.

We know that corporations and organizations in all sectors of industry emphasize efficiency. Business today is interested in the bottom line and in results. To achieve ambitious goals and accomplish the corporate mission statement, people need to work as a team toward the common good. On a more-personal level, people who wish to achieve specific career objectives realize that collaborating with their colleagues is important. However, specific behaviors sabotage the production of effective and efficient results and undermine the development of useful relationships at work and in other areas of life.

Aggression

The first ineffective way to conduct business is by aggression. Aggression, or the "fight response," is the kind of behavior that may involve screaming, pounding a desk, and yelling. The person shouts statements that typically begin with the pronoun "you"—for example, "You did this to me," "You are miserable to work with," "You are a lousy team player," "You should not be working with me," "You are the cause of all my misery," "You are the cause of my failure," and "You are going to stop me from being successful." If these sorts of statements were hurled at you, you might either run away from the situation or say to yourself, "If this person is going to be aggressive, then I'm going to be aggressive, too." That's why aggression usually achieves very little. People either retreat from you out of fear or stand their ground and become equally, if not more, aggressive. Tension is introduced into the workplace, so nothing is accomplished. No positive contribution is made toward the achievement of corporate goals. Your personal objectives are in no way advanced. And in the long term, your health is likely to suffer.

Some people, however, specialize in aggression. They attack their work. They create hostile relationships. They are belligerent with management. Their misguided belief is that if they do not approach matters aggressively, they will never get any work done and will never be successful. Furthermore, they believe that they can exert greater control over their workplaces through "a strong offense." They can grab hold of everything and everyone and "shake them into line." Once they dominate their working environments, they can forge ahead to greater heights.

Don't encourage this type of behavior. It breeds resentment, disunity, and greater hostility. It does not produce the type of working environment that is conducive to productivity.

Avoidance

Another unsatisfactory behavior is avoidance—the "flight response." People who engage in this behavior are likely to leave a meeting because they are too anxious or jumpy. Or they dodge debates with their managers or colleagues. When these people become too flustered, frustrated, or irritable, when they feel as if they are being challenged or threatened, they make themselves scarce.

Being evasive has some short-term gains. For a brief period, you elude the troublesome situation. But over the long term, this behavior is totally useless as a way of managing your affairs. Eventually, you need to face up to difficult situations. However, some people become experts at "dodging bullets." They avoid a wide variety of situations, including personal relationships that are not going well. No wonder loneliness becomes a reality for these people; they make no effort to resolve differences with other people. The sad part of avoidance is that it feels so good–temporarily–that the temptation to repeat it becomes increasingly strong. Sometimes, avoidance becomes so ingrained that the individual evades everything that is bothersome.

Avoidance can become a phobia. People who are phobic begin to think and believe that they are incapable of facing anything that is troubling to them, especially other people. What a way to live! Certain people can, over the course of time, develop this kind of pattern. They convince themselves that avoidance is not only the easiest but also the only way out. But the question remains: How long can anyone keep running away?

Passivity

Another ineffective pattern is passivity. You remain silent when you are bothered by something. Or you do nothing when a colleague has "dumped" on you. You know very well what you want to say or do, but you don't say it or do it.

People who resort to this sort of behavior are afraid to upset others. They are apprehensive about asserting their feelings and thoughts. If they express themselves openly, they might not receive approval for their actions or their climb up the ladder of success might be hindered. So they keep their mouths shut until they get so frustrated that they explode in a rage!

People who become chronically passive suffer a lot of discomfort and agitation. Indeed, the passive individual has been referred to as "the ulcerous personality." They allow their internal distress to chew up their stomachs.

Nevertheless, you cannot convince certain people to sacrifice their passivity. They are absolutely convinced that if they remain quiet and never question anything or anyone, they will be regarded as model employees and model partners in a relationship. They will be perceived as cooperative, pleasant, and deserving of a better fate.

In some cases, it might be politically wise to keep quiet. But the person who carries on this way runs the risk of being viewed as a noncontributor, as one who doesn't care or is afraid to offer an opinion. In the long run, that person will have no voice in the decision making that occurs in the work group. What is more important, he or she will be regarded as having poor communication skills. By adopting a passive strategy, the person avoids being classed as a troublemaker but may still be in trouble.

Certain individuals distort reality and delude themselves. They always believe that their way is the best way. If they are not aggressive, then they may be running away or they may be running in place, doing nothing and remaining passive.

An accountant who was having problems at work explained his predicament this way:

> I was always a gung-ho type with my work and with people. Because I approached my job this way, people saw me as aggressive. I guess I did get into more fights than anyone else. But I thought I was doing okay, until one day I received a warning from my manager to stop bullying everyone. I didn't know what to do, because that had always been my style. I got really angry and started to avoid people. If they didn't like who I was, I'd have nothing to do with them. The heck with the team approach! I could do it all by myself. But again, I got another warning, because I wasn't working well with my colleagues. What did they want from me? So you know what I did? I began to go to meetings, but I kept my mouth shut. I would do what they wanted, but I wouldn't say a thing. I figured that this was the best way to get on their good books. There were many times when I wanted to speak up, but I bit

my lip instead and kept quiet. But that didn't work either. I was so confused I gave up!

Round and Round We Go: The Pervasive Pressure Cycle

Once you become an expert at crooked thinking, you have set the stage for certain uncomfortable feelings and ineffective reactions. If you think that your health and well-being are threatened by occurrences in the workplace, which in reality are not so threatening, you will in all likelihood slip into a condition of chronic pressure and anxiety and simply ride the unhealthy merry-go-round.

This is how it works: We engage in unrealistic thinking, which produces feelings of pressure, panic, worry, or anger, which in turn give rise to inept behavior. As we continue to act ineffectively and fail to produce meaningful results at work or outside, we begin to think even more illogically. As we maintain a course of unrealistic thinking, we feel even more distress.

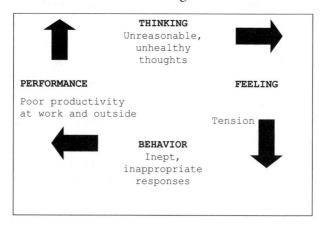

Figure 2.1   The pervasive pressure cycle

As we experience even greater pressure, we act even more ineffi-ciently. As we persist in our inefficiency, we generate more absurd thoughts. So, round and round it goes, from our thoughts, to our feelings, to our actions, back to our thoughts, and so on. These behaviors reinforce one another and set up the vicious and pervasive pressure cycle.

People tend to conclude that the cycle will never be broken. They will never achieve anything. They will always be anxious. They will always think that they are going out of their minds. They will always remain on a "pressure treadmill," bound for failure, misery, and disgrace. People get stuck in this cycle because of their inflexibility. They may stay in the same rut indefinitely, unless they begin to make significant changes.

OUTLANDISH DIVERSIONS

Over the years, we have developed some intriguing coping pro-cedures in an effort to come to grips with pressure and other unhealthy reactions. These procedures can produce some ben-efits in the short term but produce virtually none in the long term. These methods are ineffective because they do not alter the thinking processes that transform events into potential threats to one's well-being. They are merely palliative, at best. Many of these activities and strategies may be valuable in their own right. They may be enjoyable. They may be entertaining as distrac-tions. They become silly and outlandish only when they are used as techniques to eliminate pressure and anxiety.

Jogging

Many people attempt to outdistance their hassles. They suffer from the misguided belief that if they jog, whether at 6:00 a.m. or at midnight, and develop all the aches and pains that result from jogging, they will master their stress. This is grossly inaccurate. As an activity in itself, jogging is valuable. It strengthens the cardiovascular system. It tones muscles. It is useful as an aid in maintaining proper weight. It gives people a high. But as a stress strategy, forget it! I cannot tell you how many people I have encountered who jogged relentlessly, 5 or 10 miles a day each and every day, who were more fit than you or I will ever be, and yet they exhibited severe stress symptoms.

A new problem has now surfaced: compulsive jogging. If those who are driven to jog do not do so, they experience serious anxiety. Missing one or more runs adds to their stress level. Compulsive joggers not only fail to manage their stress, they may heighten it. How many people have you known who, for one reason or another, were not able to jog and went wild with frustration? They become so anxious and agitated that they are impossible to live with. Obviously, this is not the cure for stress.

Aerobics

Aerobic exercise, like jogging, is widely regarded as a panacea for pressure. It has gained popularity partly because it is reputed to flush out stress hormones. When a person experiences distress, certain hormones appear in the bloodstream. Research has shown that, once an individual exerts herself, these so-called "stress hormones" suddenly disappear from the bloodstream. This finding has led to the assumption that pressure can be controlled through aerobic exercise and other related activities. If you extend this line of reasoning logically, one would have to exercise perpetually in order to ensure that those stress hormones remain out of the bloodstream. Without continued exercise, the stress hormones might return. And they will return because they are linked to your thinking, not because you have stopped exercising.

Aerobic exercise is worthwhile as a short-term measure. Like jogging, it distracts you from your difficulties. It is great for toning and building muscles. It has been described as an aid for reducing blood pressure and lowering fat cells and sugar in the bloodstream. These are worthwhile physical results. I believe in the value of exercise, but not for reducing pressure and anxiety.

Tennis and Squash

People are scrambling all over tennis and squash courts, convinced that they can beat their pressure into submission. But, like other forms of exercise, tennis and squash have absolutely no effect on pressure. They may be fun and good exercise, but as meaningful, long-term pressure-proofing strategies, they have no merit.

Some people who really get into tennis or squash approach the game the way they approach everything in their lives: they set out to beat their opposition to the ground. If they do not win, they end up more distressed. If you go out of your way to approach these activities aggressively, you can actually bring a higher level of discomfort into your life by the insidious anxiety you experience going onto and leaving the court.

Diets

A number of people today are looking for the right diet to manage pressure. They believe that if they eat the correct food and provide their bodies with the appropriate nutrients, they will surely lead a pressure-free existence. So they reach for the latest miraculous diet on the bookshelves. They overdose on cottage cheese and fruit, pasta, protein, or carbohydrates. They try starvation. People everywhere are seeking more-novel, more-controversial diet regimens in an effort to change their lives.

Diets are often seen as magical cures. But we know that after dieting is over, people usually put back on the weight that they have lost. In fact, people commonly gain back *more* than they have lost. Consequently, they are under pressure when trying to decide which diet will work best. While on a diet, they are under pressure because they are worried about taking off weight. And after the diet is over and they put weight on again, they are even more pressured!

I would be the last to suggest that food and proper nutrition are not important. Eating a properly balanced diet is essential. However, food is virtually irrelevant to distress because it does nothing to alter your thinking.

Vitamins

We are in the midst of a vitamin craze. A vast selection of vitamins is available to help you improve your physical health. "Stress tablets" are among the most popular. People pop these pills as if they are the answer to all woes, then find that they still experience anxiety. Vitamins may be valuable, especially to people suffering from vitamin deficiencies. But vitamins do nothing to change our thinking and, therefore, do not alleviate the pressure that results from our unhealthy and unreasonable thoughts.

Vacations

Many people misguidedly believe that they can fly away from their worries. I recall counseling an airline executive who felt that she had to get away because she was suffering from symptoms of anxiety. She booked a flight to one of the Caribbean islands, believing that all her problems would disappear once she was able to take in some sunshine. After she arrived, she rushed into the hotel and up to her room, tore off her clothes, put on her bathing suit, ran to the beach, threw down a blanket and jumped on it, believing that her problems were gone forever. Two hours later, she was going crazy because she could not get away from the thoughts racing through her mind. She worried about what was going on at the office. She worried about what was happening at home. She worried about all the work she would have to do when she returned. Two days later, she booked a flight home, stressed out of her mind. The vacation had made matters worse.

Many people get more anxious when they are on vacation. I have known a few who have even had heart attacks while on holiday! Of course, a vacation can be restful. But it won't be restful if you expect it to do something it cannot do—that is, eliminate your problems!

It is true that some people are able to work out some of their difficulties while on vacation. They take the time to think and rethink their problems and formulate some concrete plans to solve them. But not everyone can do this. Some people force holidays on themselves with the underlying condition that they must relax and eliminate their problems. For these individuals, vacations may have the opposite effect of stress relief.

A restaurant owner came to see me with an interesting dilemma. He admitted that he was a happy workaholic who enjoyed the hustle and bustle of his restaurant business so much that he hadn't taken a vacation in 10 years. However, his close friends and relatives kept telling him that he was crazy and that everyone needed a holiday. They repeatedly warned him that sooner or later he would crack up. He started to worry that there might be something wrong with him. But this man simply was not interested in a vacation. He enjoyed excellent health. He hadn't been sick a day in his life. Although he didn't see his family as often as he would have liked, when they were together, they had a wonderful time. They enjoyed walking and talking, eating, and shopping together. In essence, this man enjoyed life as much as he enjoyed work. He was a contented workaholic who didn't value vacations. I congratulated him for living his life to the fullest.

Hobbies

Many individuals try to eliminate their pressure by taking up hobbies. A route salesperson whom I counseled was particularly disturbed about a rec room he was building. He had bought the best hammer, the right nails, and top-quality paneling and had set out to hammer away his stress. He would come home from a day on the road frenzied because of the hectic pace, gulp down his dinner, and run to the basement to start working on his rec room. He would then labor feverishly until midnight. He was as uptight as could be because things kept going wrong and the room was not coming together perfectly or fast enough. This is very common behavior among certain types. They approach everything, including their hobbies, in the same perfectionist way. They have to build better rec rooms than their neighbors and complete them as quickly as possible. Such a hobby can stir up considerable agitation rather than remove it, not because of the activity itself but because of the unhealthy approach behind it.

Other people try gardening, fishing, motorcycling, playing bridge, or simply reading. However, a hobby, no matter how interesting, will not lower your pressure level. It may be a wonderful diversion, but nothing more. Hobby enthusiasts have told me, "I know that I relax when I am doing my hobby." And that's great. But when the time for hobbies is over, the hobbyist has to face her problematic situation again. Take up whatever hobby you wish, but bear in mind that it was not intended for the eradication of worries!

Sleep

We have all been told to get the proper amount of sleep so our bodies will be rested enough to endure the many daily hardships we encounter. For many, sleep has become a security blanket. The truth is that sleep has virtually nothing to do with pressure.

Each of us knows that we require a certain amount of sleep in order to function effectively. We know that different people require different amounts of sleep. We also know that trying to force ourselves to rest more than we really need to can in itself create pressure. It may be that some people suffer from sleepless nights because they worry about not getting enough rest! The best advice in such cases is simply to get the rest you need. Beyond that, enjoy the waking hours.

For a few people, slumber can be so wonderful that they would love to sleep away their lives. When these people are asleep, they don't have to face their problems. But those who rely on sleep in this way still have to deal with their troubling situations when they wake.

Computers

This is the age of technology and, as such, some of us rely too heavily on the computer to distract us from our problems. Some play computer games; others get on chat lines and discuss their hardships and problems. Some search the web for pressure-related answers and come away even more confused and upset. Should I relax, should I take pills, should I see someone for therapy, should I change jobs, should I change partners, should I be more assertive and finally put my foot down, or should I walk away from everything? Quick-fix solutions rarely provide any real answers. Take psychotherapy as a viable option. If pursued, the process takes time and effort to get the desired results; it does not produce relief overnight.

Computer reliance has its own pitfalls. If we are searching for answers and don't come away with any, or come away with some that don't offer immediate relief, or we experience a sudden computer glitch in the process, "computer rage" may grip us. Computer rage is a by-product of the technology era. Pressured individuals actually take out their fury and wrath on their computers and have even been known to smash them. So computers can actually make matters worse if we have unrealistic expectations about what they can and cannot do.

Tranquilizers

Tranquilizers come in all colors and sizes. They are probably as common today as aspirin. They provide a false sense of hope and security. These drugs simply mask the symptoms of stress. When the effects of the tranquilizers wear off, people are once again faced with their problems.

On occasion, people might really require tranquilizers for a limited time. They are certainly valuable for severe and acute disorders that require temporary medication. Although they may have short-term usefulness, in the long term, they can be harmful and addictive. And although the symptoms of anxiety can be severe, trying to withdraw from an addiction to tranquilizers can be a lot worse. Nevertheless, some people become convinced of the usefulness of tranquilizers. They may even trade pills with their colleagues or next-door neighbors, thinking they are being helpful. These pills do absolutely nothing for your thinking except make it fuzzy.

Work

Work is viewed by some as an escape from their pressure-filled lives. They overindulge in their projects, meetings, and late-hour functions, not because they enjoy them but because they can get away. The hours pile up, the tiredness escalates, the lack of fulfillment soars, and the agitation mounts. The more we work, the more dissatisfied we become because things are not getting any better. Then, of course, anger and anxiety rear their ugly heads. As a consequence, we may be consumed with "desk rage," another form of attack against feelings and reactions that we have not properly addressed. People have been known to punch their desks and smash articles because of the extreme anger they feel from the misguided belief that problems will magically disappear if they are ignored.

Alcohol

We have all heard about the ravages of chronic alcohol abuse. After a rough day at work, it is not uncommon for groups of workers and supervisors to go down to the local pub and knock back a few drafts. However, this behavior can easily become a habit that can turn into an addiction. If you think pressure is bad, try coming off an addiction to booze.

These are some of the popular coping tools that people commonly use and abuse. These strategies have no long-term merits, although they may have some short-term benefits. More importantly, they do not alleviate pressure. Some strategies for dealing with pressure *do* have merit. These strategies have proved to be reliable and workable and produce meaningful results. More profound than coping tools, these pressure-proofing procedures are explored in Chapter 3.

3 Pressure Proofing by Debunking

My Mantra, Please

Relaxation can be extremely useful. During times of agitation or heightened arousal, I often practice self-hypnosis. It allows me to reduce the level of uneasiness that I may be experiencing. Once anxiety is diminished, I can carry on more comfortably and effectively. However, beyond this very important short-term benefit, I have difficulty seeing this technique as a major strategy for eliminating pressure.

There are those who would have us believe that the ideal state is one of relaxation. If an anxious individual learns to relax, this argument goes, then he or she will be able to develop a pressure-free existence. This is utter nonsense! No one can remain tranquil for 24 hours a day. No one can perform efficiently on the job while remaining completely at rest. We all require a certain level of arousal and excitement, of healthy pressure, in order to be effective. Only when the arousal level becomes too great is it worthwhile to use a relaxation method.

I recall an athlete whom I counseled. In our discussions, we talked about the merits of relaxation, as well as its limitations. It was obviously important for him to learn how to relax, but he needed to apply the technique discriminately. When he was too uptight or too nervous, he would practice relaxation. But relaxation was not a state he sought before a big game. He enjoyed being energized and psyched up for the competition. He found that being invigorated and stimulated helped his performance tremendously. The one time he tried relaxing before a game, he certainly felt tranquil and at peace with himself. But his performance was less than adequate.

Some people get even more anxious when they try too hard to relax. They demand instant results. They believe that they should be able to relax with the same efficiency that they display in performing other tasks. So, quite typically, they get even more uptight.

We have been inventive over the years, discovering a lot of weird and wonderful ways to relax ourselves. The fad one year was "pyramid power." After a hard day's work, busy people would come home, toss their briefcases aside, perhaps tear their clothes off, and place themselves under a pyramid. The idea was that, after a period of time, they would step out and be totally and completely at peace with themselves. This fad has faded into oblivion, as most fads do. But while it lasted, some people were able to brag to their colleagues that they had been helped by this wonderful structure that they believed—and the key word here is "believed"—had a mystical effect on them. Who knows? Maybe it did.

Then someone discovered the "charged particles" that were moving in the air and became concerned that an ion imbalance (too many positive ions and too few negative ions) was causing people to become uptight. This person thought that if the correct concentration of negative ions were pumped into the air, people would be more relaxed and do their jobs more effectively. Many companies purchased their own ion machines. Nothing happened. People were no more relaxed and they did not perform any better, although their environments certainly had a different concentration of ions. Certain sports teams who were performing poorly also tried ionization. As you might have guessed, after they bombarded themselves with negative ions, they continued to play poorly.

Another phenomenon was a tank used to induce sensory deprivation. If you saw the movie *Altered States,* you know what I am talking about. In the movie, the star researcher places himself in a tank filled with salt water. Once in this tank, he is deprived of stimulation. He can hear nothing, see nothing, smell nothing. He is simply suspended in water. He is left with only his thoughts and feelings. After a period of time, he drifts into a comfortable state of rest and peacefulness, which is rightly referred to as an *altered state of consciousness.* The problem is that depriving a person of all sensory stimulation for too long causes the person to begin to hallucinate. This happened to the researcher in the movie, but the story then shifted gears from nonfiction to a distinct science fiction thriller.

Some clever marketing experts made these tanks available to the public. Picture a harassed, stressed person who comes home from work and wants to relax. He strips and enters a tank filled with salt water. He closes the door behind him. He floats in the water for a while, then comes out looking like a prune. Is he any more relaxed? Maybe he is, for a little while. But he has also made himself look ridiculous. No one needs such an elaborate contraption just to get a little peace. If you want some quiet time to yourself, you can find it in the privacy of your office. If your office isn't private, you might consider going to the washroom for a short time. It certainly isn't any more ridiculous than a tank. When you find a quiet place, close the door, switch off the lights, and hold all telephone calls. Seat yourself in a comfortable chair and close your eyes. Now you have almost all the advantages of a tank, with the added advantages of convenience and practicality!

Interesting as some fads are, you might find it more worthwhile to consider some more practical techniques to induce relaxation. Examples of these procedures include yoga, meditation, biofeedback, autogenic training, progressive muscle relaxation, and hypnosis. The emphasis in these cases is not on gadgetry. Instead, you learn to control the level of arousal in your body so that you are ultimately able to bring on a restful, peaceful state.

No one procedure is necessarily better than another; each tends to produce a similar state of relaxation. Many books and articles have been written about these techniques. Find a book on one that interests you, take a course from a reputable instructor, and discover for yourself what it is all about.

It is critical that you work with a qualified practitioner, one who is knowledgeable and experienced in the particular technique you wish to use and whose credentials are clearly established. Many people claim to be able to teach these techniques but are not properly qualified. Too often people spend more time shopping for the right deodorant than for assistance that will improve their health. So take this particular shopping escapade very seriously and spend some time checking out what is best for you.

When you learn a relaxation procedure and become skilled in its use, you will have achieved a considerable goal. Ideally, you should be able to use your procedure in the office, a meeting, or other situations that are important to you. It will take continued practice, but it will be well worth the effort.

I was working with an individual who was extremely agitated, discouraged, and nervous in a variety of situations. He was jumpy in meetings. He was tense when he met people and when he had to go into his supervisor's office. It was important for him to reduce his level of arousal in these circumstances because these activities were an important part of his working day. So I taught him self-hypnosis. When he started the program, it took him approximately half an hour to bring about a reasonable state of relaxation. However, he worked at the technique diligently and persistently. With continued practice, he was able to reduce the amount of time he needed to relax himself to approximately 10 seconds. Once he became adept, he began to find that he could employ this method in meetings, in the office with his manager or supervisor, and in encounters with his colleagues. In essence, he was able to relax himself without the people around him noticing. He was thoroughly delighted with the results.

This example is not necessarily the goal to be aimed for immediately. (No doubt, certain people would strive for 5 seconds, or even less, as long as they had the lowest figure on record.) It is, however, important to practice frequently so that you can relax yourself quickly enough to deal on the spot with troubling situations, without the technique being conspicuous or apparent to anyone.

Time: Do You Manage It or Does It Manage You?

Most of us have heard about, read about, or even been exposed to time-management procedures. Time management underlines the importance of planning and emphasizes the usefulness of setting priorities. In essence, people are urged to keep a log of tasks that require completion and to order them so that the most urgent and critical jobs are finished first. This seems to make sense because it forces you to examine what you do and how you do it so you can avoid becoming overwhelmed.

Time management has been regarded as a major pressure-proofing tool because of its emphasis on time control and the regulation of work. Among other things, time-management experts have told us how to manage our phone calls effectively. They suggest arranging calls in various piles according to their importance. The first pile consists of essential calls, which require an immediate response. The remaining piles, in order of importance, could be addressed when you have sufficient time. You simply prioritize your phone calls just as you prioritize your tasks.

You may also keep an account of your activities by determining how much time you spend on each and then deciding whether you are making judicious use of each hour during the working day. If you spend too many hours on activities that do not help you meet your goals, you should put these activities aside in favor of activities that contribute to your objectives.

Time-management procedures have also been applied to activities outside the work environment. It has been pointed out that if you govern your time carefully, you will have greater opportunities to enjoy your family and friends; you will have the chance to engage in various forms of exercise and recreational activities or simply relax. Basically, time management gives you the opportunity to enjoy an enriched and balanced life. By paying close attention to how you spend your time and eliminating wasted hours, your quality of life both on and off the job should be greatly enhanced. It follows that stress will also be minimized.

However, as with any technique, there is a tendency among many people to adopt time management temporarily and then disregard it. Time-management procedures are well founded. They make a lot of sense. But they also require some mental discipline. If we act haphazardly without thinking about what we are doing or why we are doing it, we will eventually stop doing it, and that in itself can trigger worry.

We are all in the habit of running around chaotically. Eventually, we tend to forget why we are doing what we are doing or whether it is even worthwhile. A good example of this is meetings. We all know that there is value in meeting with colleagues and management to arrive at a solution to a problem or to come to a decision about an important matter. But it is all too easy to get caught up in meetings. It is not unusual to find that after one meeting, an additional meeting is organized. And then you have a third meeting about the second meeting, which was about the first meeting. Eventually you have to throw up your hands and ask yourself, "Why am I doing this?"

Similarly, it is possible to get so buried in time-management techniques that we become obsessed with arranging our schedules, coordinating our activities, streamlining our timetables, and basically overmanaging our lives. Then we get so fed up that we drop the whole thing and go back to old ways of doing business. But discarding everything makes no sense either. Time-management principles are valuable if we are prepared to use them reasonably. Think before you do!

An insurance broker described her dilemma to me:

I've always been too busy. The first week that I got into insurance, I was already up to my ears in potential business. I've been successful over the years, but I have often wondered whether I could be more successful. Maybe if I was better organized, I could write up even more business. So some colleagues and I took a course on how to manage time more effectively. It was great. Everybody raved about it. But I didn't get the results I wanted. Maybe it wasn't for me, or maybe I simply wasn't using it properly. Everything was supposed to be monitored–my phone calls, my meetings, my discussions with people, my "cold calls," my meal breaks. I spent so much time keeping track of everything that it cut into my selling time. Then I began to ask myself why I was doing this. It's really not like me to be so picky and precise and plan every detail of my life. I got so frustrated that I dropped the whole thing! This move ended up being the right one for me.

To value the reflective and introspective process as much as, if not more than the action process, is important on both an individual level and a corporate scale Whether you are introducing time-management practices, new methods of entrepreneurship (or "intrapreneurship," which is entrepreneurship inside the organization), new management techniques, or improved communication methods, it is still important to step back and examine motives. Contemplation often clarifies the goals and reasons for following through on a particular enterprise. If you think before you act, you are likely to act much more effectively. If you reflect before you implement time-management procedures, you are likely not only to benefit by their use but also to use them over a longer period. If after thinking about them you decide not to use these procedures, you will be able to discard them knowing you have made a reasonable and considered decision.

Debunking Those Nutty Thoughts

Earlier we discussed the damaging effects of unhealthy thinking, or thinking that produces pressure. If thinking is critical in producing anxiety, it is also critical in pressure proofing. Thinking that is unrealistic, unreasonable, unproductive, and ultimately unhealthy can be changed to become reasonable, productive, and healthy.

You are in control of how you reason! If you have created your own silly thinking, then you can "uncreate" it and construct something else in its place. More realistic thinking will minimize your distress and pressure proof you against any change that comes your way.

In an earlier section, I described a number of typical thoughts guaranteed to drive you nuts. Now I propose to take these nutty ideas and create more reasonable ones. This is the essence of debunking. If you adopt this approach, you will find it much easier to manage your work, feel better about yourself, and become more productive. You will notice that you get along much better with your colleagues, management, friends, and relatives. You will perceive a greater sense of well-being. Most important, you will manage your pressure!

MISTAKES HAPPEN AND NOTHING TERRIBLE OCCURS.

If you make a mistake, the world will certainly not come to an end. For some perfectionists, this concept is quite an eye-opener. We all stumbled before we learned to walk. We all stuttered before we learned to put together a proper sentence. If we can accept the fact that we learn from our mistakes, then we can acknowledge that it is not so terrible to make them. But there are those who believe that you must get things right the first time or forget it. Don't forget it; learn from it.

An aside: One of the most important things that we can do as parents is to teach our children how to fail. If we allow our children to explore their environments, make mistakes, and fall flat on their faces—and in the process, point out that it is not terrible to fail—our children will not fear failure or crave perfection as adults. Too often we demand too much. We demand perfection when it comes to schoolwork. We demand that our children get things right. If we took the approach that we can all learn from our blunders, then children could handle their so-called "failures" more easily.

The same intolerance exists regarding mistakes in the workplace. No person ever receives a pat on the back for making a blunder. It's rare that an individual receives a kind word for learning from a failure. But we know that nothing awful will result if we do make an error. There may be some heat directed our way, but that typically subsides, especially if we make the necessary corrections the next time. Only if we continually and regularly repeat the same errors are we likely to run into serious trouble.

THERE ARE CLEARLY NO RIGHT AND WRONG WAYS TO DO THINGS.

What is right for one situation or person may not be right for another. There is a lot of gray area between black and white. We all know that, in the world of business, few rules are carved in stone. If we accept this and work with it, life in the workplace becomes quite a bit easier.

Some employers might argue the point. They might claim that the bottom line is always the determining factor, no matter what! But it's not so simple. Making a profit unethically, for example, or to the detriment of the customers or clients, is not something to aim for. Sometimes, short-term gain can lead to long-term loss. Just look at Enron! So once again, it is important to examine our thinking and strive to use our best judgment in an exciting environment that, I believe, is built on a foundation of risk-taking and entrepreneurship, not on a groundwork of right and wrong.

I WILL ACCEPT CRITICISM AND LEARN HOW I CAN BENEFIT FROM IT.

This also means that I will keep my mind open to feedback. If the criticism is constructive and it makes sense to me, I will take it seriously enough to attempt to act on it. On the other hand, if the criticism is destructive and does not make sense to me, I will accept the fact that my critic is entitled to his or her opinion. This thinking, surely, is quite a bit more reasonable and realistic than fearful thinking. Criticism does not necessarily have to be equated with failure.

If we could also teach our children to accept criticism, in the same way we should teach them to accept mistakes, they might be a lot healthier and happier. Certainly these children, as eventual adults in the workplace, would perform and produce far more effectively.

I WILL NOT DEMAND APPROVAL.

No one needs approval in order to do his or her best, although it is certainly nice to receive it. There is no rule or regulation that stipulates you have to receive "positive strokes" each and every day in order to be productive. If that were the case, no one would be producing in the workplace. Certain people regard approval as they do food and drink: they think that they need it to survive.

Some management-training experts might disagree. They feel it is important to offer positive feedback and approval, especially when work is well done. I have no quarrel with this. As a psychologist, I understand the merits of positive reinforcement. If you complete a project successfully, it is certainly nice to receive support and approval. However, there is a difference between appreciating approval and demanding that you receive it from everyone around you. People who demand it but don't receive it are in deep trouble. They end up needlessly stressing themselves. They also draw all sorts of negative conclusions about how poorly they must be doing because they did not receive their quota of positive strokes. This ends up hurting their productivity.

Many individuals in the workplace find it difficult to give positive feedback. Do not jump to conclusions about your performance if you do not receive the approval you believe is your due. When you do receive endorsement, enjoy it. But realize that there is no assurance that you will continue to receive approval, and it is important that you not demand it.

I WILL NOT DEMAND THAT I BE COMPETENT, BUT I WILL CERTAINLY STRIVE FOR IT.

There are many people, the perfectionists, who seriously and earnestly believe that they must be unfailingly competent at everything they attempt; otherwise, they are outright failures. Hardly anyone is competent at everything, but it doesn't follow that we are all failures. It simply means that we are more capable at some activities than at others. We can certainly strive to be skilled at everything we try, but if it doesn't work out, the world won't end. When people carry the thought around in their heads that total and complete competence is critical, they set themselves up for some uncomfortable discoveries.

It is one thing to accept that we are fallible and quite another to believe that we have failed miserably. In fact, the way in which we are judged is quite complicated. Work performance and competence are not the sole determinants of how we are rated. Subtle elements, such as social skills, people skills, and other intangibles, enter into a rating of one person by another. The rating is often more subjective than objective. So why get hung up on it? It is much more sensible to think: "I will accept the fact that people will not always see me the way I would like to be seen." You have no control over how others view you. It is in the hands of the person who is carrying out the rating, whether it be management, colleagues, or friends. The priority for you, as a person, is simply to do your best each and every day. Then, more often than not, things will work out the way you wish them to. And isn't that pretty good? You might wish to be rated as perfect. But perfection is an illusion. And since we are talking about healthy and reasonable thinking in this case, illusions have no place.

I WILL NOT BE FEARFUL IN THE PRESENCE OF AUTHORITY.

You *can* challenge what people say and do in a constructive fashion and nothing catastrophic will happen. This is a major problem for certain people, especially those in administrative functions who perform clerical duties. Administrative employees are among the most pressured groups. All sorts of ideas run through their minds, many of which are unrealistic and unreasonable. They believe their supervisors and managers are like gods and are afraid to challenge them. And yet they go around complaining, griping, and cursing the day they came into the workplace. They complain not to the people who are important but to their colleagues. If their thinking were more reasonable, they would approach their managers and supervisors and talk things through.

You can approach people in authority and work out your disagreements. You can present your ideas in a constructive fashion. Doom will rarely result. This is not to say that you have a written guarantee that everything will turn out just the way you want it to. But in most cases, things will probably work out. You are not likely to be fired or demoted. And you may discover that the person in authority appreciates your input.

While we understand that communication in the workplace is important, we still experience communication breakdowns and still foul up. We assume that because we are knowledgeable in communication skills, strategies, and techniques, we will obtain what we want from those we work with. We assume that if we express ourselves openly and let our feelings be known, our colleagues and managers will take note. When the expected results are not forthcoming, we throw up our hands in frustration, anger, and indignation and say, "The heck with this."

Clerical and administrative staff are notorious for this. When they get up the nerve to talk to management and management does not give them what they want, they withdraw, muttering furiously that they will never communicate what they feel again. Such people give up too easily. They demand results from just one exchange. Dialogue is ongoing. Communication is never-ending. Ignoring that the channels for talking and negotiating are open most of the time is another example of thinking that inevitably leads to frustration.

I ACCEPT THE FACT THAT LIFE IN THE WORKPLACE IS NOT ALWAYS FAIR AND JUST.

This means that neither your colleagues nor your manager have to agree with what you say. For many people, this is very, very difficult to accept. But let's face it: things are not always equitable and impartial. And if they were, it would not necessarily imply that the people you work with have to pay attention to you. This is reality!

You can argue that you're not going to stand for it. You can swear that you're going to make it better, more fair, more just. But you can't, can you? Maybe a few individuals have the power to create an environment just the way they envision it, but most of us mere mortals do not. If you demand this power, you are putting yourself in an awkward and stressful position.

In actuality, a workplace that does *not* respond instantly to one person's idea of what is just is more likely to be productive than one that does. There are benefits to disagreement. Some of the best solutions result from controversy. Those who insist that their workplace be calm and settled and that everyone concur with them have unrealistic expectations. Constructive controversy or "creative tension" can be meaningful and productive.

I GIVE MYSELF THE RIGHT TO BE OUT
OF CONTROL ONCE IN A WHILE.

This means that you will not always be alert or brilliant. After all, do you know anyone who is always alert and brilliant? Even presidents and prime ministers have their bad days. Yet there are people who persist in demanding perfect control from themselves. They pigheadedly believe that only if their conduct is flawless will they be successful, productive, and pressure-free.

There is no question that people like to take charge of their lives. People appreciate knowing what they need to do in order to excel at their jobs. But to believe that they have to perform in a dazzling manner in order to get ahead is stretching it. They can only strive to do their best. If their performance is not splendid, then at least they did their best. That, surely, is something to take pride in.

The issue of control seems to be central in any discussion of pressure and anxiety. Some people have been led to believe that if they are in control of their lives, they will experience no distress. On the surface, this seems to make a lot of sense. But what happens when, for whatever reason, they are unable to rule their activities in the way they believe they should? Say, for example, that an individual has not met a target date for the completion of a particular project. Or, a person ends up feeling bored on the job. What are they to do? Well, certain people go to pieces. They start to think in terms of doom and gloom. They begin to believe that their productivity will deteriorate until they hit rock bottom.

If you tend to think along these lines, why don't you make work easier for yourself? It is very appealing to think that you can take charge of your working life, but you can't always. If you permit yourself the luxury of being tolerant of your own occasional, unintentional errors, it takes the pressure off. You might think, "I won't be as productive" or "I won't be as successful." In fact, you will be even more successful and more productive and will achieve your goals more often. Instead of focusing on being in control at all times, you will be focusing on what you want out of life. That means directing your attention to your objectives and what you wish to achieve.

I CANNOT ANTICIPATE OR BE CERTAIN OF EVERYTHING.

Some individuals seem to think that it is necessary to be a step ahead of everybody else. They have to know what is going on not only in the minds of their managers but also in the minds of their colleagues. If they are a step ahead, this will surely guarantee prosperity!

Of course, the difficulty is that it is not always possible to determine what is going on in people's minds. Still, some people seem to think that they are so intuitive or perceptive that they can second-guess everybody. Many claim, for example, to be able to read people's "vibrations." They believe that they have a sixth sense that makes them capable of reading nonverbal messages, voice intonations, and facial expressions. Clearly, these "readings" are nothing more than guesswork, but there are those who actually base decisions on them. Then they are dumbfounded when things don't work out the way they expected. It is important to respond to what we see and hear, but even the most perceptive observer can't predict too much for certain. Even meteorologists talk in terms of the chances of rain or the probability of snow. Isn't life really one big probability?

I ACCEPT THE FACT THAT I WILL NOT ALWAYS GET WHAT I WANT, ALTHOUGH I WILL CONTINUE TO STRIVE FOR IT.

In other words, if things don't come your way as quickly as possible—i.e., the good salary, the beautiful office, the prestigious position—you won't be heartbroken for the rest of your life. Some people tend to be immune to such reasonable thinking. However, acceptance of this sensible thought makes life quite a bit easier. It certainly makes it possible to contain pressure symptoms.

People who demand everything from life and expect to get it all immediately are obviously in for a big disappointment. An individual may be fortunate enough to experience a string of successes. But if she goes on to believe that this string will continue for the whole of her career or life, she has made a major thinking error. The fact that four consecutive items on her "to do" list worked out as planned does not ensure that items 5, 6, and 10 will work out, too. Some people are not prepared for this reality, and they run into trouble.

I have heard individuals say, with complete conviction, that if they are not demanding on the job, they will never get what they want! Allow for the fact that things might not always be the way you want them to be.

I WILL GIVE OTHERS THE RIGHT TO BE WRONG AND WILL NOT BE ANGRY OR HOSTILE TOWARD THEM.

This thinking makes a lot of sense, but to certain people, mistakes are intolerable. They believe that when people make errors, they deserve to be punished. Not surprising, they are also angry and hostile toward others. This attitude does not make for cooperative relationships in the workplace. The notion of teamwork is very important in today's workplace But how can we expect to get teamwork from a person who is always judging other people? Some individuals constantly set themselves up as judge and jury to those around them. They are constantly on guard to see who goofs and who does not. In their view, those who slip up are fallible and those who are not absolutely efficient should bear the harshest consequences.

Accepting that you are imperfect makes it easier to accept imperfection in others. There are those who say that if you put up with anything less than perfection, you will never be a success. This is not reasonable or realistic. People who try to do their best, to be as productive as they can, will nevertheless have occasional slipups. Why condemn them? Why be angry and hostile toward them? It makes life a lot easier for you and your colleagues if you accept your own and other people's mistakes. This principle may sound almost spiritual or religious. I view it as a certain philosophical style that aids in reducing and mastering stress. Acceptance, tolerance, patience, allowance for imperfections: All these terms have to do with your outlook and with your thinking and are critical in controlling stress.

**IF I DO NOT RECEIVE FULL SUPPORT AND ENJOY
A CARING ATTITUDE FROM PEOPLE AROUND ME,
IT WILL NOT BE THE END OF THE WORLD.**

When some people are not as productive or as successful as they believe they should be, they cry the blues and expect everybody to be sympathetic. If they do not receive this sympathy, they begin to hate everyone and to loathe their work environments. This kind of reaction is damaging to the individual and to work morale. If things don't go right on the job, for whatever reason, it would be great to get consolation from others, but what if it doesn't happen? Well, some people get more miserable and discouraged and, finally, become more anxious. They formulate silly conclusions. For them it is proof positive that the world is mean, rotten, uncaring, unresponsive, and miserable. This is complete nonsense.

Colleagues, supervisors, and managers will not always come across the way that you expect. Why not realize that? Why not give up that demand? If things don't work out on the job for one reason or another and people are not overflowing with condolences, it is unfortunate but not the end of the world. Maybe tomorrow your colleagues and friends will be more sympathetic to your cause. But you must realize that concern and care are not like food and drink. You do not need them to survive. If others choose to be considerate (and some will), enjoy it. But if they are not, it doesn't really matter.

I ACCEPT THE FACT THAT I WILL NOT FEEL SUPERB ALL THE TIME.

Certain people demand that they feel great each and every day. By "feeling great" they really mean that they must never get anxious, worried, jumpy, tense, or stressed. Is this realistic? Of course not. But when some people are not feeling just right, they start to panic. They begin to brood. They worry about not feeling well. Then they worry that they are worrying about not feeling well. Sound mixed up? It is! This is what pressure is all about. Why get into this vicious cycle? We are not machines; we are human beings capable of experiencing the full range of emotions. This is what makes living and working so exciting: the ups and downs, the challenges, the defeats, the victories, and so on.

If you demand that you feel only up, happy, ecstatic, joyous, exuberant, ebullient, energetic, and zestful, isn't your goal going to be rather difficult to achieve? It certainly would be exhausting! So get your thinking in line. Be a little more flexible and pragmatic. Allow for the full range of human experience. With luck, you will feel reasonably well and be reasonably productive most of the time. But if you get hung up on feeling on top of the world all of the time, I can almost assure you that you won't be very productive. You will be too worried about not being 100%.

I WILL NOT JUDGE MYSELF ACCORDING
TO WHAT I DO OR DON'T DO.

When a person's performance is judged, it is *only* the performance that is judged, not the person's worth. However, people are notorious for thinking that if their performance isn't what it should be, they must be complete misfits and failures. Things are fine when their performance appraisals are good, but all hell breaks loose when their appraisals are unsatisfactory. Just because a person receives a mediocre or poor performance appraisal for a certain period does not mean that he should renounce his status as a member of the human race!

When your work is reviewed, you have an opportunity to think about your performance and make the improvements that are necessary. If you are obsessed with the rating that you receive, you will not pay attention to the corrections that need to be made; instead, you will focus on how rotten a human being you must be. If you concentrate on that, you will be pressured and anxious. So leave yourself alone. Management has the right to judge your accomplishments. It is part of their function. Work with the appraisal but don't draw conclusions about yourself. Draw conclusions about your productivity and try to improve on it.

I WAS NOT PROMISED A CORPORATE ROSE GARDEN.

Work is not always rewarding, and colleagues and managers are not always considerate, kind, and respectful. Doesn't knowing this make life in the workplace a little easier? Doesn't this take the pressure off you? Now you can be more flexible and roll with the punches. When your work happens to be gratifying and stimulating and your colleagues are cooperative and attentive, you can rejoice. When work is not as fulfilling and your colleagues are not so accommodating, then you can tolerate that, too. It will be possible for you to work through mundane projects, handle less-satisfying tasks and details, deal with uncompromising colleagues, and not get so hung up about it.

IT IS NOT TOO LATE FOR ME TO CHANGE.

You alone are responsible for your life and career. You are capable of recognizing changes that need to be made in your behavior and of making those modifications if you wish to. Why do you think performance appraisals have gained such prominence in the workplace? They provide a major opportunity for managers and supervisors to sit down and discuss problems with the people receiving the reviews. Together, they can talk about what has and has not been accomplished. Granted, these sessions are not always objective but, with luck, they are enlightening most of the time. More important, if people are reasonable enough to consider the feedback that they receive, then they can make calculated decisions about what changes to make. People who always complain, who are cynical, and who reject change are the ones who experience pressure. Those who let it be known to colleagues and management that they are open-minded and adaptable and are prepared to consider other ways of doing business can only be admired by those they work with.

An actuary whom I counseled offered a revealing commentary:

> My career and my life in general were always filled with rules and regulation. There was a right and a wrong way to do things. Basically, I thought that living should be an exact science. In other words, if I did something, then I believed that I should get a certain reaction. For example, if I worked very hard to complete a particular project, then my manager should applaud my efforts, reward my accomplishments, and sing my praises for a job well done. Boy, was I let down!
>
> Also, I was a chronic perfectionist and a chronic worrier. What a combination! I was truly unhappy. I was always asking myself if this was the way I wanted to be for the rest of my life. And I always came up with the same answer: No. After all, how many lives did I have?
>
> Yet there was a choice: I could continue to drive myself into the ground, or I could change. So I dedicated myself to doing things differently. I made a point of not worrying. I made a point of accepting that I wasn't perfect and my work wasn't perfect. I made a point of accepting that not everyone approved of me and of the work I did. I made a point of believing that I could only do my best and, after that, let the chips fall where they may. You know, it made a tremendous difference. It was as if a big load had been removed from my shoulders. What a relief! I felt much better. Now I enjoy life. Also—and this is really funny—my work is better and I get along better with people.

If you can adopt and subscribe to reasonable, rational, and realistic thinking, it sets the stage for a profound reduction in your anxiety. Remember, if pressure originates in the mind, it is there that you have to look first for solutions. If you debunk the nonsense and make these necessary shifts in your thinking, you will find that pressure can be contained and controlled, to the point where you can manage your working life effectively and efficiently.

POSITIVE AFFIRMATIONS: A BOON OR BOONDOGGLE

A psychological trend that continues to flourish in the workplace is "positive affirmations" or "the power of positive thinking." You may have read books about it. You may even have experimented with it and found that it did not produce the desired results. In fact, positive thinking may actually increase pressure. This may sound like a major contradiction. You would think that once you start to think positively, pressure would be eliminated because it has to do with negative, unhealthy thinking. Replacing negative thinking with more-positive thinking should be the answer. However, this is not always the case and, in a number of situations, positive thinking makes matters worse.

Positive thinking, or positive affirmations, came into prominence because some people noted that those who performed poorly were cynical, pessimistic, gloomy, and dismal. Thus, it was believed that teaching these pessimists to think with optimism, inspiration, and promise would turn their performance around so that once again they could proceed on the road to success and achievement. If people regularly repeated optimistic statements to themselves, thought very positively, and looked to the future with buoyancy and enthusiasm, they would experience extraordinary improvement both at work and elsewhere and life would be rosy. This concept seems logical on the surface.

However, once you closely examine the reasoning, you can begin to see the cracks and flaws.

Many sports teams are big on positive affirmations. It is not unusual to find athletes in the locker room before a big game psyching themselves up. They might say to themselves: "I am going to be dynamite. I am going to perform fantastically. I am going to destroy my opposition. I am going to play the greatest game I ever played in my life. I am going to win." After they repeat these expressions, they run onto the field or the court or the ice and expect miraculous things to happen. They assume that once they have said positive things to themselves, they are bound to perform positively. But as we know, one team wins and the other loses, although both may have used positive affirmations.

Let's take an example: Sally works for a placement agency and is a good employee. She has been doing well on the job over the years. Lately, however, things are not working out. She is stressed. She notices that she is jumpy and irritable, not the calm and efficient person she would like to be. One day, Sally finds out about positive affirmations and she starts to engage in this practice. Every morning she wakes up and repeats the following messages to herself: "Today is going to be the best working day ever. Today I am going to meet all my deadlines. Today I am going to get along with everybody. Today I am going to impress my manager. Today is going to be the most fantastic day I have ever experienced. Furthermore, I am going to be in complete control.

I am going to feel wonderful. I am going to think clearly." After saying all of this, she feels very psyched up.

Once Sally has recited all of those encouraging expressions to herself, what happens when she comes to work and events don't develop the way she thought they would? How will she react? How is she going to feel? You might suggest that if things don't work out, it's because she didn't think positively enough. But that is not true. It happens sometimes that people do think positively, but the world doesn't cooperate. Circumstances in the workplace do not fall into place. Sally may be unnecessarily causing herself a lot of grief by truly believing that just because her outlook is extremely optimistic, everything will work out positively. Can we really predict how things are going to work out? Can we really forecast how we are going to get along with people? Can we really determine how management is going to react to us? Can we really foresee with certainty that all of the project deadlines will be met? No! So do not place yourself in this particular bind. Even soothsayers cannot predict everything, especially everything positive, that will occur. With hard work and a bit of luck, good fortune may come your way, and you will be rewarded for your efforts. But there is no guarantee.

Of course, this isn't good enough for those who are determined to adopt positive thinking and make it work. And when positive things don't materialize, these people ruin themselves psychologically. They experience more anxiety than ever before. They used this positive thinking, which they believed was so

powerful, and it didn't even work! They take this to be unequivo-
cal proof that they will be distressed for the rest of their lives,
they will never succeed, they will never amount to anything, and
they will be doomed for eternity.

Positive thinking has some merit because it heightens your
arousal. It does psych you up; it mobilizes your energies and gets
you prepared for the working day. But it does not guarantee positive results. Nor does it necessarily eliminate pressures. What I
am suggesting, therefore, is that you recognize the limits of the
procedure and use it with some caution.

SELF-TALK IS OKAY

Remember how people used to say that if you talked to yourself you were a little bit nutty, but if you answered yourself
you were really nutty? Things have changed. Now we have
legitimized internal dialogue, or "self-talk." Since we are prone
to unhealthy thinking and because we now understand that
unsound logic is a key contributor to our pressure-packed lives,
it's okay to talk to ourselves and challenge what is going on in
our minds.

How do we do this? Let me offer you some questions that
you can pose to yourself. Your responses to these queries will
make it possible for you to confront your illogic, counter your
faulty reasoning, and call into question your poor judgment.
This process should help change your thinking so that you come
up with a more reasonable and realistic perspective.

The next time you get extremely wound up, ask yourself the following questions:

- What thought just went through my head?
- Does that thought actually make sense?
- Is there any evidence to support that thought?
- How do I know that thought to be true?
- What evidence is there to disqualify that thought?
- Does that thought contribute to my health?
- Is that thought helpful?
- What thoughts would be more helpful and realistic?

If you consider these questions carefully, you will quickly realize that there is not much evidence for your particular thought. The idea does not make much sense. It is not realistic. Knowing this, you can work on replacing your illogical thought with a more sensible and rational one.

Can you begin to see what is happening? You are becoming your own counselor and challenging your thinking as it has never been challenged before. You are overturning the reasoning that caused your severe pressure. In doing this, you should be inspired to generate more-credible and well-founded thoughts to replace the unreasonable ideas that have plagued you for so long.

When you are extremely wound up, you can also ask yourself the following question: "What is the worst thing that can happen to me?" In answering this question, you will begin to appreciate that nothing too terrible is likely to happen. No catastrophe will occur. Your life will not be threatened. Your well-being will not be jeopardized. Your career will not be totally and completely damaged. Developing this healthier perspective has a tremendous impact on your level of upset.

The superintendent of a school board once offered these words of wisdom to me:

> Do you know how I manage pressure? I argue with myself. I debate with myself. I examine my logic to determine its sense, suitability, and rationality. You see, I have a very active mind, which sometimes gets me into real trouble. But I also have the capability to change what goes on in my head. Often my colleagues find me walking down the halls mumbling to myself. But it works. First, I talk to myself and come up with a more reasonable outlook on the particular matter at hand. Then I decide whether I need to do anything different. In a way, I've become my own therapist, and I don't even have a Ph.D. in psychology!

Other questions that you can ask yourself are, "Where is it written that I have to do this?" "Why does life have to be this way?" "Why should that person act that way toward me?" In responding to these queries, you will soon recognize that no rules are "carved in stone." You don't have to do this or that. People do not have to behave toward you in a certain way. Work does not have to offer the ultimate in perfection and reward. Again, you can begin to appreciate that this self-talk is very worthwhile because it is loaded with common sense, solid logic, and profound realism.

Getting involved in this question-and-answer thinking will have a favorable impact on your health. Try to become an expert at talking to yourself. Ask yourself questions that probe, investigate, and explore the ideas that you believe in, that comprise your philosophy, and that have brought you pressure and grief. Then try to come up with reasonable answers. When you have worked out your answers, adopt them as your new philosophy; embrace them as your new way of viewing the workplace. Once you have accomplished this, and have made a habit of doing this, you will learn that pressure is manageable and you are indeed pressure-proofed.

Seek Not Outside Yourself, Success Is Within

Mary Lou Cooke

We all have imaginations. Some of us use them in weird and wonderful ways. Others use them to create pressure rather than relieve it. People who are pressured commonly develop powerful mental pictures of doom and gloom. They contrive traumatic images and fabricate imaginary catastrophes. Their minds seem to spawn scenes that contribute to their anxiety.

Let me give you an example: A situation that provokes a great deal of worry for many people is public speaking. Many people dread making presentations to their colleagues and managers. Skill at public speaking has a pretty good payoff. If you are capable of making good presentations, you are likely to receive praise and positive performance appraisals; you might even be considered for early promotion. But people who are disturbed about the prospect of making a presentation usually have frantic imaginations. They visualize a scene that is bound to upset them and may ultimately hurt their chances of delivering a satisfactory talk. They might, for example, picture themselves as somewhat jumpy a couple of days prior to the talk. They see themselves finding it difficult to sleep well, eat regularly, and socialize with others, particularly with people at work. They visualize themselves working very hard at the presentation, yet not feeling assured. On the morning of the presentation, they picture themselves feeling very upset. They may be nauseated, unable to eat breakfast, unable to get dressed properly, lacking in confidence. Outside the room just before the presentation, they envision themselves as extremely nervous and agitated. They imagine themselves repeatedly rehearsing in an effort to increase their courage, yet still finding that they are extremely anxious. They imagine being in front of their audience, with shaking knees, trembling hands, quivering voices, and spinning heads. They see themselves reading through their presentation with great difficulty. Afterward, they envision themselves fumbling with the questions posed to them and struggling to the point where they are simply unable to answer. They picture themselves walking away from the meeting with their head down, feeling like complete failures. Furthermore, they hear colleagues saying that their presentation was poorly organized and inadequately delivered and that the speaker was inferior, inept and second-rate.

If you conjure up images like this, you will more than likely experience considerable distress and find it difficult to do anything. Rather than carry out a presentation, you would probably want to lock yourself in your bedroom and stay there! I am not suggesting, however, that it is impossible to deliver a presentation or perform any other function unless you have the appropriate pictures in your mind. What I am suggesting is that if you pay attention to the images in your head, it might be possible to reduce your pressure and improve your performance. People who complain about extreme anxiety when giving a presentation typically create these stressful scenarios. So not only are these individuals severely wound up, they can't do their jobs. If you visualize yourself crumbling when giving a talk, it can become a self-fulfilling prophecy. Your actions conform to the pictures in your mind. Certain people have become experts at picturing the worst. Then they wonder why they're doing so badly.

If we can use our imaginations to hurt ourselves, we can also use them to help. That is why today, more than ever before, a great deal of emphasis is being placed on the power of the imagination. In baseball, football, tennis, and many other professional sports, athletes are being trained by sports psychologists to use their imaginations more effectively. Psychologists are telling athletes that if they prepare themselves properly, using their imaginations, before they perform or compete, they will probably perform more successfully.

You might think that using the imagination in this way is a repetition of positive thinking, but there is a clear difference. Positive thinking involves repeating positive affirmations and phrases to get emotionally charged up in order to perform better.

Using your imagination involves not words, but images. A series of performance-enhancing images is used to prepare the body for the real action that is to take place. It is hoped that the performance will be improved, but again, there is no guarantee. Did you understand? There is no guarantee! If you think there is, you may be in for a big, uncomfortable, and unwelcome surprise.

For example, skiers are encouraged to visualize themselves moving down the slopes just the way they have always wanted to. They are told to picture themselves holding their bodies in comfortable positions, keeping their skis properly angled, taking the hills smoothly, making the turns with ease, generally skiing at their best. After preparing themselves in imagination, they can then attempt to actually ski down the hill. People who are afraid to go down a slope are encouraged to visualize it first. Why? Because it prepares the body for the activity about to take place, and it relieves the anxiety and worry associated with trying something new.

Many Olympic athletes are using visualization and achieving tremendous results. I once watched two high jumpers at an indoor track meet. Before running down the runway and trying to leap over the bar, each would stand at the foot of the runway for a brief period of time. While they were standing still, I saw their heads in motion as if they were moving along the runway, then coming to the bar, moving over the bar and finally landing. They carried out this exercise three or four times. Only after they completed the exercise in their imaginations would they actually sprint down the runway. These athletes, by the way, were considered to be the two best high jumpers in the world.

If the imagination is a powerful tool for athletes, it can certainly be useful as a device for people in the common workplace. To return to the dilemma of people who are troubled by presentations, what if they trained themselves to use different images? It should make a significant difference. Here is what troubled individuals could picture: A couple of days prior to the presentation, they could imagine themselves putting the final touches to the upcoming talk. They could visualize getting excited about the opportunity to lead a presentation about some aspect of their work. The night before the presentation, they could envision rehearsing the talk. They could imagine eating a good breakfast on the morning of the talk, then jumping into the car and driving off to work feeling confident that they will do their best. They could picture themselves in the meeting room just before the talk, arranging their notes at the podium and watching the crowd shuffle in. They could imagine themselves looking out at their audience, feeling relaxed, comfortable, and at ease. Then they could imagine themselves presenting the material in a logical, explicit, and entertaining fashion. While speaking, they could notice that their bodies were relaxed and their minds undisturbed. After the presentation, they could visualize themselves handling questions with ease. For queries that they were unable to answer immediately, they could imagine saying, "I don't know the answer to that, but I will research it and get back to you." They could envision themselves leaving the room, feeling good and looking forward to their next presentation.

If you visualize these images, you will feel considerably better than if you imagine the set of disturbing pictures previously described. If you are tense about an upcoming presentation, these images will help lessen your nervousness. Your imagination is a powerful resource. By visualizing scenes in which you try your best, you train yourself to control your anxiety. So use your imagination regularly. You can resort to it prior to embarking on any activity that you feel troubled about. Picture yourself performing the task just the way you want to. If you rehearse these scenes over and over, you will perform more effectively and, at the same time, minimize the anxiety that was previously associated with the task.

However, there is a potential trap in all this. There are those who are notorious for thinking that if they imagine events in a certain way that is how they will work out. We must realize that there is no guarantee of this. Visualization is worthwhile, if you realize its limitations as well as its usefulness. If you rehearse scenes in your imagination and picture yourself doing the best job you can, there is a reasonable likelihood that you will carry out the task effectively. But there are no guarantees that your experience will be just as you imagined. If it isn't, you should be prepared to learn from the experience. Most important, you can incorporate what you learn into your images, so that the next time you use your imagination, you will visualize a number of new scenes in preparation for an even better effort. The key point to remember with this procedure is not to envision yourself performing your tasks perfectly. Perfection is unattainable, so just visualize yourself doing the best job that you can.

This procedure works for athletes because they picture themselves in a reasonable light. Skiers don't imagine themselves going down the slopes perfectly. High jumpers don't imagine themselves jumping previously undreamed-of heights. They simply visualize themselves doing what they are capable of doing, namely their "personal best," to get the results they want. When it comes to activities in your workplace, do the same thing. Imagine yourself performing in such a way that you achieve the results you seek. Once you become really adept at using your imagination in this fashion, you will find that you can accomplish tasks more easily and also feel considerably better.

There is another way to use your imagination. This method involves talking to yourself in a reasonable fashion while visualizing certain troubling images. Let us return again to those employees who are bothered about making presentations. With this approach, you picture that which you are afraid of and worried about. You imagine standing in front of the audience, about to give your talk. You are feeling nervous, jumpy, anxious and pressured. In the midst of this, you ask yourself: "What can I think and say to myself that will reduce my tension so that I can get on with my presentation?" You then carry on a dialogue with yourself. You might repeat certain questions and answers. For example: "What is the worst thing that can happen to me if I blow this presentation?"; "Well, management and my colleagues might not care for this talk." "Where is it carved in stone that I always have to do things perfectly?"; "Well, I can only try my best, and if it doesn't work out, I will try to learn from my mistakes. No one loses their job for learning from mistakes." "And if I finally come to the conclusion that I am not a great presenter can I live with that?" You might continue this self-talk until your level of disturbance is considerably reduced. Once you have rehearsed this sequence a number of times, you will be ready to try the real thing and you will be less upset when you present because you have prepared yourself psychologically.

With this approach, you use your imagination to picture the worst, while simultaneously talking your tension away. With the previous method, you used your imagination to visualize helpful images. Which method is better? Try both, and use the method that works best for you. The main goal is to use your imagination more effectively. Can you picture the results you would get with a sensible approach to your career and your life in general, combined with a productive imagination? Wow!

4 Shaking Things Up

If You Do What You've Always Done, You'll Get What You've Always Gotten

Up to this point, we have been talking mainly about the influence thinking and imagination have on the creation and reduction of pressure. But your actions are also important. Typically, people who are experiencing tension end up mismanaging their lives. Individuals who are anxious simply do not perform well. Constant worry interferes with their daily routine and ultimately hampers their careers.

Given that our thinking has changed, and we are now using our imaginations to our advantage, the next step is to consider doing something different. If we are mismanaging our working lives, then it is time to figure out how we can perform more effectively.

SELF-DECLARATION

The first thing to do is express yourself. Certain people know nothing about assertiveness. They either get very angry, aggressive, and hostile, or they withdraw and complain abut their terrible environment. Self-declaration is quite unlike aggression. Aggression usually involves shouting, yelling, desk pounding, and using the classic word "you," as in: "You cause all my problems," "You are a pain in the neck," "You are no good," "You never do things right," "You are always in the way," and so on. Using the word "you" in every expression either drives people away or causes them to react aggressively toward you. If you are trying to work as a team and cooperate with others in the workplace, you are going to have problems.

The two key ingredients are the words you use and your willingness to negotiate with other people. Rather than prefacing every sentence with "you," use "I": "*I* believe this," "*I* think that," "*I* would like to try this," and so on. What you should then add to your "I" communications are closing statements such as: "What do you think?" "What do you believe?" "What would you suggest?" "What would you like to try?" and so on. When you begin your statements with "I," it becomes very difficult for the person you are dealing with to construe your discourse as being aggressive. You are simply stating your thoughts and feelings, then inquiring about the other person's view. In that way, you invite the other person to express his feelings and thoughts.

You are not trying to overpower or attack your colleague; you are simply trying to work out your differences.

WIN–WIN NEGOTIATION

Your willingness to negotiate is another matter. This is not only a matter of the words you use; it is a guiding principle. Once you adopt a bias toward negotiation, you need no longer see your colleagues as a threat or your supervisor as an enemy. Instead, you will view these people as members of the same organization who, in their own ways, are trying to fulfill their responsibilities. Occasionally, differences of opinion, approach, and goals arise. This is the time for negotiation, not aggression—and the type of negotiation where both parties come out winners. Win–win negotiation simply means that "one party does not get the entire pie; rather, both parties get a piece of the pie."

There is a trap here, too. Certain people believe that if they are expressive, they will get what they want. There is no guarantee of this. You can easily start to think that because you have learned to be self-expressive, everything will come your way. Colleagues will be nice to you. Management will be considerate toward you. You will get everything you ever wanted from your job. Of course, this is unrealistic and unreasonable. It is important simply to declare yourself, whether you get what you want or not. It is important to take the time and energy to put on the table that which is bothering you. Even if the people with whom you work do not listen to you, at least you have been able to get it out in the open. Tension often relates to people's inability to convey their feelings and thoughts and what is bugging them. If you get into the habit of self-expression, at least you will know that you tried. That in itself is tremendously valuable.

You should find that once you become assertive, more people will cooperate with you. You should also find it considerably easier to work with others. And, very important, people will seem to respect what you have to say more often.

Dialoguing

Self-declaration also serves to establish grounds for effective dialogue. This means that it is important not only to express yourself but also to listen to, share with, and support the other person. This may seem very foreign to those who have no time for other people because they believe they are the only persons who know what they are doing. They think it's a waste of time to talk to others and simply get on with work.

It is critically important to engage your colleagues and managers in regular dialogue. In many workplaces, the chief complaint among people is that there is too little communication. That is not to say that people do not know how to dialogue with others. The problem more often is the unwillingness of people to set aside time to talk and share. Those individuals who, unfortunately, find this practically impossible will pay the price.

Make it a personal goal to interrupt your working day with a few communication pauses. When the opportunity arises, take advantage of it. This doesn't mean that your entire working day should be spent chattering to the person beside you. But a number of brief exchanges can go a long way toward fostering an atmosphere that makes you more productive and less stressed. By all means, talk about how you are doing but, equally important, pay attention when the other person tells you how she is doing.

Once you become adept at engaging others in dialogue, you will be known as a person with good "people skills." Such recognition can be useful. The person who is successful today possesses not only solid technical skills but also solid communication skills. You're not wasting your time by communicating; you are investing in your career!

CREATIVE PROBLEM SOLVING

It is also useful to work on your creative problem-solving skills. This may sound simplistic. Doesn't everyone naturally know how to solve problems? However, today, more than ever before, organizations are acknowledging the importance of specific problem-solving skills and are attempting to ensure that their people acquire and apply them to their everyday tasks. These creative skills basically involve identifying problems, breaking them down into specific challenges, generating a variety of potential solutions, evaluating the solutions, determining the best solution, and implementing it. There are many variations on this basic approach. If you are uncertain about your natural ability to solve problems or think that you could use some retraining, many programs are available. As with any course you take, however, make certain that you shop around for a reputable program and trainer. Don't be surprised if your manager comes up to you one day and asks you if you would like to enroll in a company-sponsored program. More often than not, you will be expected to participate. Remember, every organization is looking for an "edge." Effective problem solving may be exactly what they—and you—need.

RISK TAKING

This is the age of the entrepreneur and the "intrapreneur." Both have in common one characteristic: the ability to take risks. Whether this means taking risks with particular projects or taking risks with particular people, the same basic principles apply. They can be summarized as follows. To take chances successfully,

- Do not be afraid of failing
- Do not demand perfection
- Do not demand guarantees

Certain individuals don't take chances because they want guarantees. They want to know that everything is going to work out. They want to know that people are going to treat them well. They want certainties in life.

Instead of uncertainty, successful risk takers see opportunity, adventure, experiment, events that pose a challenge to their traditional ways of doing things. This, for them, makes the workplace exciting. However, certain people never take risks. They base their lives on strict predictability and security. When their expectations are not met because they won't take a chance, they drive themselves nutty and experience severe pressure!

Taking risks also includes experimenting with new ways of doing things. Risk takers are willing to consider new forms of dialogue, namely self-expression and assertion, or new methods of problem solving. They are willing to take the chance that their experiments may fail. They may talk more directly and openly to people than they ever have before. They may deal more forthrightly with their managers about what is troubling them and how to correct it than they ever have before. They attempt to break down old routines that contributed to their nerve-racking patterns of behavior.

So, try something new, something different, without knowing if it will work out. If you never take a risk, sooner or later you will kick yourself for not having tried!

Risk takers are also willing to be embarrassed. To fail, to be unproductive, to be disapproved of, not to be accepted by others—all these outcomes may give rise to embarrassment. Unless you are prepared to chance embarrassment, you will find it very difficult to take risks.

If you do happen to fall flat on your face and are embarrassed, then what? Certain people tend to feel that the world has ended. But it hasn't. How long does the uneasiness last? A lifetime? Of course not. It is temporary. But if you are controlled by your discomfort, it will be virtually impossible to do anything different. Only if you refuse to be dominated by your fear of embarrassment and shame are you free to experiment in life.

In order to confront your discomfort, it can be fun and interesting to purposely create embarrassing situations for yourself. Think of something silly that you did in the past and how uncomfortable it was for you. Do it again! This may sound absurd, but if you can do something that produces embarrassment and withstand the uneasiness, you will learn to bear embarrassment with very little pain. Then you will no longer be controlled by that fear.

Here are some simple exercises that can help you to deal with embarrassment and thus make it easier for you to take risks. They will cause you some uneasiness, but the consequences will not be so severe as to hurt your stature or career in the organization.

Experiment 1: The Elevator Trick

The next time you are riding the elevator in your building, turn around so that your back is facing the door and you are facing the other passengers. Say "Good morning" to them. You may also want to smile. This exercise will prove to be somewhat embarrassing for a number of people, because most people in an elevator stare at the floor or at the numbers that indicate each floor. They rarely look at the other passengers. Enjoy the uneasiness until it dissipates. Also pay attention to what you told yourself to help it dissipate.

Experiment 2: The Illiterate Report

If you are accustomed to reading and rereading reports that you have prepared in order to correct every single spelling and grammatical error, go out of your way to submit a report without rectifying the mistakes. This is not to say that you should do this for the rest of your career. Just do it once or twice with the sole intention of making mistakes and suffering some of the discomfort that arises when they're pointed out to you. Then pay attention to how long the embarrassment lasts and the debunking and self-talk that reduced its intensity and duration.

Experiment 3: Memory Lapses

Another interesting exercise is to purposely forget a colleague's name. Think of someone whom you have befriended and trusted for a considerable length of time, whose name you know as well as your own. Then, the next time you bump into that person, pretend to forget her name and proceed to ask her what it is. You will find that this makes you feel uncomfortable, but the embarrassment will be temporary.

Experiment 4: The Volunteer Guide

Here is another experiment. If you happen to take a subway, bus, or streetcar home from work, when the vehicle comes to a halt to let passengers out, stand up and call out the name of the stop. People may think you're strange. On the other hand, they may appreciate the comic relief. But you know as well as I do that whatever they think about you, they will soon forget. Your embarrassment will last only a short time.

Work is boring for some people because they do things the same way every day for fear of taking chances. If you start to take more chances, life on the job and outside will be more meaningful and more rewarding.

It's Not the Mountain We Conquer But Ourselves

Sir Edmund Hilary

So far, I have described a number of techniques that, taken together, will make it possible for you to effectively reduce your anxiety. These techniques are tools that, when used regularly, will give you the capability to be an efficient and a resourceful "pressure-proofer" in the workplace and outside.

When you experience symptoms that you recognize as tension, stop doing whatever you are doing. The first thing is to be aware of what your body is telling you. It is time for some peace and quiet. Because you may be feeling anxious, agitated, jumpy, or nervous, it is important to relax. Use the method that works best for you. You may picture a soothing image or repeat to yourself certain words or phrases that have a calming effect. You do not need to spend a long time on this. If you have been regularly practicing a specific relaxation technique, you should find that you are able to settle yourself down quite quickly.

Once you are relaxed and have reduced your level of tension and anxiety, you are better able to think clearly. Now you can decide what situation upset you and what problem you want to work on. Then ask yourself what went on in your head and what you said to yourself that got you so upset. In other words, what unreasonable and unhealthy thoughts did you create that made the situation difficult for you and made you extremely tense?

Once you have determined what you said to yourself to produce the pressure symptoms, challenge those thoughts. Start a mini-debate with yourself. Question your unrealistic and unreasonable thinking. Challenge yourself with some real vigor, and make certain that you come up with something more logical and more sensible. Produce thinking that is tied to reality, not fantasy, in order to formulate more reasonable thoughts. This is the process of debunking.

Now you can use your imagination to help you visualize the solution to your problem and the steps necessary to get there. When you are thinking more clearly and sensibly and have a picture in your mind of what you are after, you can begin to consider what you are going to do to get there.

First, it might be important to identify the actions that did not get you what you wanted. In other words, work out what behavior was ineffective. Then be sure to do something else. Try doing the opposite of what you have done in the past. Risk doing something different so that you break an old, ineffective habit and replace it with new behavior that is more effective and efficient. Risk changing your behavior so that you become more competent and achieve the results you are after. Finally, think about some key people on whom you can count for support and assistance if needed. This sometimes heightens the chance of success.

Only Those Who Dare to Fail Greatly,
Can Ever Achieve Greatly

Robert F. Kennedy

When you find yourself in a stressful situation, remember the simple, effective processes discussed in this section. To summarize:

1. Stop.

If you are under severe pressure, abandon whatever you are doing.

2. Relax.

Calm down so that your mind is free from distraction.

3. Think.

Identify the unreasonable ideas that precipitated your tension.

4. Debunk.

Challenge your unreasonable ideas. Replace them with ideas that are more realistic and helpful.

5. Risk.

Break the old habits of behavior. Try something new.

6. SUPPORT.

Seek assistance from people who are willing to help you.

Hold yourself accountable by rewarding yourself for new actions taken (e.g.., buying yourself a new article of clothing, going to a favorite restaurant) or punishing yourself for procrastinating (e.g., cleaning your house, burning a $50 bill).

The process of debunking is truly an exciting one. It empowers you to challenge illogical, panic-ridden ideas and replace them with more reasonable ones. In a sense, you are developing a personal approach to your emotional well-being. By realizing that pressure is linked to unrealistic thinking and that pressure-proofing is connected to realistic thinking, it becomes possible for you to take charge of your health. You no longer allow pressure to overcome you; instead, you overcome it through the process of debunking and the constructive actions that follow.

Pressure-Proofing Roadmap

Here is your roadmap to helping you resolve your problems and increase your health and well-being.

Record the issue you want to work on. Be specific. The questionnaires in the Appendix at the back of this book may be helpful. Complete as many as you need to help you decide the key issue that requires your attention.

_____

_____

Record the debunking you use to counteract your unhealthy thinking about the issue that triggered your tension.

_____

_____

Record the healthy thoughts and self-talk you use to overcome your problem.

_____

_____

Imagine you have just solved your problem. Record where you are and what you are doing. Be precise. This becomes the solution you now go after.

Record the new behavior and actions that you will take to achieve the solution.

Action _____ by date ..../..../....

Action _____ by date ..../..../....

Identify people who will help and how they will help you.

Person _____Helpful action _____

Person _____Helpful action _____

Two

Singing the Workplace Blues

5 Diagnosing the Blues

The Risks of Relentless Pressure

Being under relentless pressure for a long period of time can lead to the workplace blues and can result in depression. Currently, depression is the fastest growing emotional problem in the workplace, as absence rates and prescription drug usage indicate. More people on the job are taking selective seratonin reuptake inhibitors (SSRIs), the newest family of antidepressants, than ever before.

There are a number of signs and signals that let you know you are in trouble. However, the best way to illustrate the problem is to relate an actual life story related to me by a university professor whom I was counseling.

> I was raised in a really good home. I basically had everything I wanted as I grew up. I had a lot of friends. I remember a lot of happy times. My schooling went reasonably well, so I decided to go on to university. I scored exceptionally high grades in university. As well, I established many friendships and some close relationships. Even-

tually I graduated with honors. Everyone had a lot of high hopes
for me. With my good grades and my family's connections, I was
assured of a very attractive career.

I quickly settled into a meaningful job. I secured an outstanding
position at a major university, with the promise that there was a bright
future ahead of me. While I was beginning to fulfill some of my career
ambitions, I met a wonderful man. I fell madly in love with him. We got
married and had two children—a beautiful boy and a darling girl—who
fulfilled all of my parental dreams. To complete this apparently ideal
family, two dogs were added. So I had my career, the man of my
dreams, and the children I always wanted. We were like some Hollywood ideal of family life, like the Cleaver family on "Leave It to Beaver."

Added to this beautiful family were all the traditional trappings.
We lived in a large five-bedroom house, had two imported cars in the
driveway, wore the most stylish clothing, and ate at superb restaurants.
In essence, we led the life of an upper-middle-class family. We didn't
have the problems which beset many average families—no financial
concerns, no marital difficulties, no problems with the kids. You might
think that I would be delighted and happy for the rest of my life.

I should have had absolutely nothing to worry about. But something was missing. Nothing seemed to matter anymore. If a new project
came up at work, I was not excited about it. When my kids came home
to share their excitement with me, I found it hard to care. I was often
exhausted. I simply did not want to work so hard anymore. When I was
around my colleagues I was fed up with them. My department head
was a pain in the neck. In fact, everyone I worked with was a pain in
the neck. I didn't want to be with them anymore. If I could have taken
a flight to some deserted island and stayed there for the rest of my life,
I would have done it. I wanted to remove myself from all the trials, the
tribulations, the responsibilities, and the cares that accompany the roles
of professor, spouse, parent, and so on. I was burned out!

You might say in reading over this account, "This sure sounds
like me at times." In fact, it is safe to say that many people have

experienced feelings very similar to the feelings expressed in this story. Does this mean that everybody has the blues or is depressed? What does it really mean to have serious workplace blues? The signs and signals include:

- Irresponsibility
- Exhaustion or fatigue
- Lackadaisical attitude
- Little concern for the job and fellow employees
- Anger toward colleagues and supervisors
- Cynicism
- Abdication of responsibility
- Lack of motivation
- Poor appetite
- Disrupted sleep pattern
- Isolation from friends
- Withdrawal from relatives and immediate family
- Quarrelsomeness
- A strong desire to do something extreme and break from tradition
- Depression

The blues involve the depletion of your resources, both physical and psychological, stemming from a compulsive desire to achieve. This is caused by exaggerated expectations that you believe must be fulfilled and that are typically, but not always, job-related. Unfulfilled expectations bring on an overwhelming tendency to cynicism, pessimism, and negativity.

Am I A Candidate for the Blues?

Ask yourself these questions:

- Do you find that you are tired and totally exhausted after a day's work, although you are not really overworked?
- Do you find it hard to tolerate people at work?
- Do you notice that it is difficult putting up with family members and their demands?
- Do you lack motivation to get involved in your favorite activities and hobbies?
- Do you feel like dispensing with all of your responsibilities?
- Do you find yourself complaining more often about how badly you feel?
- Does the future look grim to you?
- Do you get the strong impression that no one really knows or cares about what you are going through?
- Do you find the basics of living—such as eating, sleeping, and socializing—not important any more?
- Do you get the feeling that if the world stopped turning today you would jump off?

If you answered "yes" to many of these questions, you are clearly a candidate for the blues, if not depression.

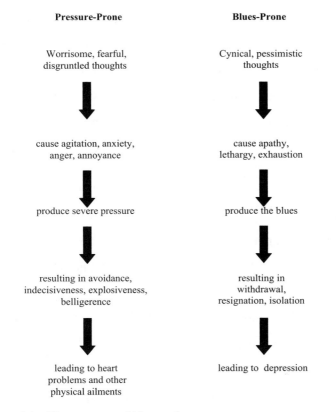

Figure 5.1   The pressure and blues pathways

PRESSURE VERSUS THE BLUES

The basic difference between feeling pressure and feeling the blues is the thinking associated with each. The person feeling the blues thinks in very cynical, pessimistic, negative terms. This person is morose and glum and maintains a dreary, dismal outlook. This individual is completely fed up with work and life and has lost the energy and enthusiasm to do anything about it.

On the other hand, the person feeling extreme pressure thinks in very anxious, worried, and aggressive terms. This individual is always fearful that something terrible will occur. At the same time, this person doesn't want others standing in the way of success; otherwise their ultimate nightmare might happen—failure. So this individual angrily sets out to work around, work over, or work through people.

FROM PRESSURE TO THE BLUES

There is no doubt that you can move from feeling extremely pressured to feeling the blues by a shift in thinking. When worried, fearful thinking changes to persistent cynical, negative thinking, there is a good likelihood of the blues occurring, possibly ending in depression. Certain people make this transition in thought because things aren't working out, success isn't coming fast enough, mistakes are too frequent, people aren't cooperative, or management isn't accommodating. When success is delayed, these negative thinkers begin to believe that success will never come their way, people will never listen to them, and they will never amount to anything.

A model whom I saw for counseling complained about a rash of symptoms that she couldn't explain. She informed me that her symptoms had changed and she couldn't figure out why. She really thought she was going mad. Even as a little girl, she had always dreamed of becoming a *Vogue* model. She looked after herself; she dressed well; she kept fit and trim. She went to the best modeling schools. She began to get a few small jobs here and there, but the big breaks weren't coming her way. She began to worry a lot. Maybe she didn't look good enough? Maybe she didn't carry herself well? Maybe she didn't get along well with people? Maybe people didn't like her? Maybe she would never be a *Vogue* model. She always found herself on edge. In fact, she would often blow up at friends and relatives over insignificant things. She picked on people close to her and would even blame them for her misfortune. Then, one day, she woke up and it didn't matter any more. She stopped caring. She believed that she would never make it. Luck was not on her side. She would always be a mediocre, small-time model and nothing more. So she gave up. She stopped pursuing potential opportunities. She stopped seeing close friends. In essence, she had burned out!

The Blues Profile

The blues seems to be a sickness of achievers. It typically plagues those with lofty beliefs. It torments those who possess inflated ideas about how the workplace should be, how much they are going to contribute, how fantastic their working relationships are going to turn out, and how successful their careers will be. This is not to suggest that having high expectations is a disease worse than death. But when you are committed to lofty expectations, you may have a problem when they do not come to fruition. Victims of the blues typically commit themselves body and soul to meeting and fulfilling these extreme hopes. Furthermore, they stubbornly and pigheadedly refuse to lessen their demands, to lower their expectations.

Blues sufferers typically demand that their careers offer them more than most careers are designed to deliver. They seem to trust that their work will make their lives far more meaningful, their marriages enriched, their characters more worthy. But what job can do all this? Those who trap themselves into believing that their careers can make it all happen for them typically find that the payoff from their work is not equivalent to what they dreamt it would be.

Victims of the blues lead very restricted lives. The only thing that is important to them is their work, and they are compulsively driven to work to the exclusion of everything else—people, activities, everything that interferes with their performance and their career. As a result, they are very boring. If you ever talk to these characters, you will find out that the only things they talk about are their jobs, the projects they are currently working on, or the ones they plan to work on. If you discuss anything but their jobs, they tune out, space out, and switch off. They simply do not care to listen. You may find these people at parties, social functions, dinners, etc. always engaged in a discussion about work. If you mention anything about the arts, the sciences, sports, relationships, movies, whatever, they are gone, mind and soul. As soon as you return to the topic of work, they come to life. It is almost as if you plugged them into an electrical outlet and the lights in their heads went on again.

GENDER

Some other features of blues' victims are noteworthy. Today, women more than men seem to be suffering from the blues. This is a provocative phenomenon, but not really inexplicable. An increasing number of women are actively competing in the workplace. They are interested in careers and management positions. Because of their intense desire to make it, women (like many men) may develop inflated and extreme expectations regarding their careers and their contributions to society that may be completely unreasonable. When these expectations are not fulfilled, they suffer no less than men in the same situation. Ultimately, they experience the blues and possibly depression.

This phenomenon affects women returning to the workplace and, most of all, those women entering the workplace for the first time. These novices seem to be most extreme in their expectations. This is not to say that women should not enter the workplace or strive for success. Women must be in a position to compete and give it their best. But when extremely high expectations and uncompromising demands are not fulfilled, the blues become a distinct possibility. Another factor affecting women in particular is the very real and continuing domination of many industries by men hostile to women's aspirations. Such barriers are undoubtedly difficult to overcome. If a woman expects and demands that she surmount every hurdle and fails, she may be in trouble!

Some men have become familiar with the blues and benefited from their experiences by lowering their demands and toning down their extreme ideals. Other men may have learned from conversations with their male colleagues that they had better get rid of their exaggerated expectations. Such encounters, in individual cases, may have reduced the chances of the blues.

At her first job, a recent graduate was shocked to find "tradition" standing in the way of her progress. She also discovered depression standing in the way of her health:

> I stood top of the class when I graduated from the MBA program. I expected every door to be open when I entered the job market. Sure enough, I landed a job with a top-notch company. My friends warned me that this organization was conservative, but I thought, "What do they know?" When I was hired, I was told that I would be placed in a high-potential group with other MBA grads. We were all keeners. We worked like animals and loved it.
>
> Although I was the only woman in the group, I believed that it didn't matter. But my manager regularly reminded me how lucky I was to hold a position that had always been held by a man in the past. But I knew that I was doing well. In fact, I outperformed my five male colleagues. I knew it, and management knew it. Yet when a promotion came up, to my amazement, one of the other members of the group got it.
>
> I was furious. I ran in and confronted the manager. He was blunt. He said that I would have to be more patient because the company wasn't used to having such a high-powered woman around who demanded so much, so soon. He also said that I would be promoted, but that it would take a little bit longer. I couldn't believe my ears. I

thought this kind of nonsensical thinking went out with the horse and buggy. This was the first time I'd ever experienced discrimination disguised as tradition. I knew all about the laws surrounding discrimination. But it wasn't so clear-cut, because the manager claimed that my colleague deserved the promotion. But I deserved it more. I wanted that promotion and that's all there was to it. The company had no right to obstruct me this way.

I began to get down on myself and everyone I worked with. I became very angry, cynical, and withdrawn. I didn't feel like facing anyone at work anymore. I even began to stay away from work. In essence, I became depressed, another mental health statistic. Fortunately, I had some close friends point out that I had gone too far. They spent an entire weekend with me, repeatedly telling me that I couldn't change the world overnight. Also, they told me that I was hurting myself. If my health was important to me, I would need to be more constructive. So I continued to work at the company, although I eventually left for a better position.

AGE

Younger people seem to be experiencing the blues more than older people. This makes sense when you think about younger employees who come straight out of school. They may be men and women who excelled in university, were accustomed to getting good grades, and were told that they were outstanding scholars. They come into the organization prepared to set the world on fire. In essence, they expect to be superstars. When their grandiose notions are not fulfilled, they become disillusioned and frequently burn out.

Older employees are typically more experienced, have been with the company longer, and are wiser—not in the sense that they are more intelligent but that they may have been disillusioned at one point. They have realized that it is important not to be so demanding. This realization allows them to tolerate being unfulfilled more easily. They don't drive themselves nutty or experience the blues as frequently.

Some young people these days jump from job to job, hoping that they will come across the perfect position. Why? Because their extreme ambitions and aspirations are not satisfied as quickly as they expected. They are constantly frustrated. They are scrambling around, desperately yearning for the position they always dreamed about. Are these people wasting their energies? Will they remain in a constant state of unfulfillment? Certain employees do, indeed, devote their lives to a search for something they may never find. This journey of disillusionment is sad because a lot of energy is squandered and a lot of talent is lost.

MARITAL STATUS

Divorced and single individuals appear to suffer the blues more than married people. One explanation for this seems to be that people who are on their own often throw themselves into their work. After a divorce, people often jump into work with both feet. This behavior is legitimate, certainly, if you don't get carried away. But some divorced people work day in and day out. The more they work, the more they expect from work. Because their marriages were not satisfactory, they expect to get all their satisfaction from work. Every personal failure, every personal inadequacy must be overridden by the success that they will have to derive from their careers. So they begin to establish lofty and exaggerated aspirations that they must fulfill in order to compensate for the rotten lives they led with their partners. They need to make some kind of contribution to society through their careers since they couldn't do it through their marriages.

No doubt it is important to spend time in a meaningful way, especially if you have just been through a divorce. Work and productivity give one a sense of accomplishment. Individuals take pride in doing a good job. But doing a good job can never heal the pain and the wounds that people experience after a divorce. No career can actually eliminate the personal concerns, reservations, and uncertainties about future relationships that develop. Work alone can never guarantee that an individual will be regarded as an outstanding member of society. No career is likely to turn an individual into a better human being.

Still, there are those who firmly believe that their careers will keep them sane. When their fantasies and personal demands are not realized, they begin to set themselves up for eventual problems. Remember, work is not designed to turn your life around or correct relationship problems. Work can be exciting and meaningful, but it has its limitations. It is not your entire life. If you act as if it is and carry with you a whole variety of bizarre and extreme expectations that must be satisfied, you are in deep trouble.

Some single people also have an outlandish approach to work. The ones who run into the most difficulty, however, are those who find it especially difficult to form close relationships. These individuals jump into their work as if it were a last resort. Work must give them all the happiness, glamour, glory, and success that the rest of their lives has not been able to provide. Those who bring these attitudes into the workplace are in for a big and unpleasant surprise.

Married individuals are less likely to suffer from the blues than divorced or single people. All sorts of explanations might account for this difference. But basically, their expectations, especially those related to work, may be more moderate and less demanding. Married people are also more likely to be occupied by other interests and activities. Inasmuch as that is the case, they may not place as much emphasis on the job and what the job must do for them. Because they may have more reasonable expectations of their work and career, they are less likely to experience serious problems. Of course, not all married people are shielded from the blues; some have extreme expectations not only about work but also about their families. They have exaggerated expectations about their marital relationships and how happy they must be, about their children and how bright and well-adjusted they should be, about their pets and how many tricks they must perform, and so on. When married people get this wound up, they may end up suffering from "double blues": blues on the job and blues at home, with depression likely to follow.

The Revolving Blues Door

The blues cycle begins with our value system. Our values, principles, and ideals obviously influence our behavior. And our behavior determines the likelihood that we will end up in the revolving blues door. Two key influences have a direct and indirect impact on our value system: society and family.

SOCIAL VALUES

What does society tell us? What sort of ideals does society reinforce? What are the subtle messages society offers that we in turn assimilate? In no uncertain terms, Western society has tended to make it clear over the generations that we, as individuals coming into the workplace, must rise above our parents. If our parents achieved a certain level of success in their careers, we must surpass them. After all, is this not what progress is all about? In addition, we must work extremely hard each and every day of our lives. When we work to achieve excellence in the workplace, we will gain the respect of our community. Being successful in our careers is critically important. As we continue in our drive toward excellence, we must acquire prestige, status, and security. If we accomplish all this, then we will truly be happy and content.

Society has had an even greater influence on us since the onset of television and computers. Both have taught us to go after the good life. We are in the "now generation": Who knows? We may not be around tomorrow.

Education and affluence have taught us to reject the simple ways of doing things in favor of more complicated lifestyles. We must have the best clothes. We must have two cars in the driveway, both imported. We must have a big house. We must have everything that is available—DVD players, compact disc recorders, personal computers, iPods, Palm Pilots, cell phones, and mini-TV screens in our cars. If you do not achieve excellence and success, you may end up with only a few toys. Your life will be too simple. So you will have to push much harder if you really want to enjoy yourself and be truly happy.

Society has also made it abundantly clear to us that we must be "sexual gymnasts" today. We must experience multiple orgasms or consider ourselves mediocre lovers. You should try harder to make lovemaking as interesting and as complicated as you possibly can. Because isn't that what lovemaking is all about? You have to become the greatest lover ever. Only then will you be truly happy in your relationships.

Furthermore, we have been led to believe that all relationships must be filled with romance and happiness. If our marriage is not overflowing with romance and happiness, then it may be time for a divorce. In fact, some experts in the field of marriage and divorce tell us that, in the future, we will go through a series of marriages, all based on contracts. Prior to getting married, you will sit down with your partner and negotiate a contract. The contract might state that after 5 years have passed, the marriage is "null and void" unless both parties wish to negotiate another contract. If you look your partner in the eye and feel like running away, you will terminate your contractual marriage and go on to the next. This process might be repeated five, six, or seven times during a lifetime. This is not so far from reality: There are currently many couples who marry only after they have negotiated a marriage contract, or "prenup."

Today, in order to excel as we feel we must, many people feel that it is important to work twice, three times, four times as hard. Good examples of people with this mentality are professional athletes. A reporter points a microphone at an athlete after an important game and asks: "You had a great game today. How did you do it?" The athlete solemnly replies: "Well, today I went ahead and I put out a 1,000% effort on that field. I really did it. I pushed myself beyond my limits and I just simply got it all together. I was superhuman today!"

Viewers watching the interview might then say to themselves: "Gosh! I haven't even tapped my potential yet. Look at that athlete, and how much he put out. He put out 1,000% and was fantastic on the field. Maybe I can stretch myself and go beyond my full potential. Maybe I can put out 1,000% and be just as successful as he is." Once, putting out your best simply meant giving 100%. Now, however, the message is: "Go beyond your limits, go beyond your potential, go into that realm of the 1,000%." Not surprisingly, when people who are accustomed to putting out 100% strive for 1,000% and don't reach their goals, they join the ranks of the blues and maybe the depressed generation!

After you have driven yourself to distraction, you may be too exhausted to enjoy anything. In this state of lethargy, you may end up experiencing the "Peggy Lee syndrome." If you have ever heard that great jazz performer sing the song "Is That All There Is?" you know what I am getting at. When you are too exhausted to enjoy anyone or anything, you may ask yourself: "Gosh! Is that all there is to life?" After you have tried desperately to get all the possessions you should have, after you have stretched yourself beyond your limits, after you have worked maniacally to beat the competition into submission, and made yourself crazy in the process, you may scratch your head in wonderment. You may finally sit down and ask yourself: "Was it all worth it?" And some people get depressed when they realize that it wasn't.

I recall talking with a publishing executive who "wanted it all":

> I promised myself and my family that we would have everything we ever dreamed of. I began to work three times as hard as before. If I worked really hard, I knew the returns would eventually come. I was doing well but not well enough to have the two Mercedes Benzes, the 5,000-square-foot home with a four-car garage on an acre of prime land, the servants, the indoor swimming pool, and the trips each quarter to exotic places around the world. So I pushed myself even harder. In the process, I virtually forgot about my children and my wife. I abandoned my friends. I was driven to fulfill my promise at all costs. But the results were still not commensurate with my efforts. I started to drink excessively. I started to take tranquilizers. Eventually, I got

extremely depressed, yet I didn't know why. My family and I finally sat down one memorable evening and asked ourselves what we had done with our lives. The plain facts were revealing and devastating.

FAMILY VALUES

Not only is society influential in shaping our value system; so is the family. Your family tells you, in no uncertain terms, that in order to succeed, you have to pull yourself up by your bootstraps and get on with it. In the process, be sure that you trust no one but yourself. It is a mean, cruel, wicked world out there, and all the people in it are out for themselves. Therefore, the only person in whom you should have faith is yourself. In essence, we have been taught to be paranoid, to constantly look over our shoulders to make certain that no one stabs us in the back.

Families also point out that it is important that we persevere at all costs. Never accept defeat. If we suffer a setback, we must overcome it and move on to the final goal: success.

Equally important is to make sure that we never admit weakness to our colleagues, managers, friends, or relatives. If people know about your weaknesses, they will surely take advantage of you. So keep your feelings and thoughts to yourself. Make certain that you project a positive image at all times. Make sure that you are in complete control and that no one really knows you. This will guarantee your success.

Families also make it clear that the worst thing we can ever do is let them down. If we happen to fail, we carry not only the guilt of personal failure on our shoulders but also family-inflicted guilt.

Finally, families have drawn up the eleventh commandment. This commandment is: "Do the right thing." And what is the right thing? The right thing is to succeed. The wrong thing is to fail.

In describing the influence of society and family on our value system, I may have overstated and embellished the case. But these standards and values do permeate our lives, overtly or covertly. They affect our daily conduct. They have a powerful influence that we need to recognize. They are the reason that so many people are so unsettled and frustrated at work. Anyone would be flustered and unnerved if they had to live up to these standards. This, in the extreme, is what the blues and ultimate depression are all about!

Pathway to the Blues

Going from the blues to depression is a process of progressive emotional deterioration. It can be roughly described as consisting of four phases. In reading the description, you might think that you have to go through this succession of levels to burn out. This is not the case. You don't have to start in Phase 1 and progress to Phase 4. Depending on how distorted and unfulfilled their demands and expectations are, some people can experience the fourth and most severe level almost immediately. However, I present the process in phases to demonstrate how the blues can develop in seriousness and intensity. Clearly, it is important to identify the symptoms and intervene as early as possible, in order to halt the course. Otherwise, the problem becomes more severe and requires more time and greater effort to work out.

Picture Mary, a bright, enterprising, excited law graduate who is ready to start work. It may be her first job or a new job that she is looking forward to. Mary is ready to go. But in addition to her enthusiasm, she has many values buried in her mind that will shape what she expects from the job. They will also determine how she behaves on the job.

PHASE 1: HOT TO TROT

Mary enters the workplace and begins to experience Phase 1, the "eager-beaver" stage. She is loaded with hustle, spirit, and ambition and says to herself things like: "I must handle everything," "This job must do it all for me," "I have to make this world a better place," "I must overcome and conquer all," "I must be a true success," "I must achieve excellence." In short, her thinking is grandiose. She is overly zealous and too idealistic with respect to what she hopes to accomplish. We see a very single-minded and purposeful individual who is bound and determined to succeed at all costs. This person is consumed by energy, drive, and tremendous appetite for glory.

PHASE 2: DISENCHANTMENT

As time goes on, exaggerated demands and expectations go unfulfilled. Mary then drifts into Phase 2, disillusionment.

She is beginning to realize that the job simply is not measuring up to her expectations. However, she knows where the answer lies——in good, hard work. If only she works longer and harder, everything will be fine. Although she is disoriented, confused, and impatient, she knows she must push on. She knows that she must put out more than 100%. While she is scrambling around to overcome her disillusionment, she is irritable and has lost some of her confidence, but she is still consumed by the burning desire to overcome adversity and excel.

PHASE 3: FRUSTRATION

As time and lack of fulfillment continue, Mary eventually drifts into Phase 3, frustration. Now she realizes that the job may never measure up. She becomes more desperate, angry, and short-tempered. She begins to blame others for her misfortune. Throughout this stage, she becomes increasingly exhausted. She is losing her enthusiasm for the job. At the same time, she is becoming more cynical and callous. She withdraws further from colleagues and management. Attendance at important meetings is the last thing on her mind. As she moves through this stage of frustration, she loses more confidence. Gradually, she realizes that the job is not going to work out.

PHASE 4: DESPAIR

As time and unfulfillment maintain their steady course, Mary eventually drifts into Phase 4, despair. Now she knows that everything is over. Her expectations and dreams will never be realized. There is a tremendous sense of failure, apathy, dishonor, and disgrace. Isolation, loneliness, helplessness, and hopelessness are the order of the day. She is drowning in a pool of misery. When she wakes up in the morning, she feels like pulling the sheets over her head and staying in bed for the rest of her life. She experiences a tremendous urge to run away and abdicate all responsibility. If this process continues, Mary will probably end up being severely depressed. The ultimate outcome of the blues is, in fact, a classic state of depression.

During my hospital experience, many patients passed through our mental health services, experiencing the basic signs and symptoms of a depressive disorder. Our team of experts—which included psychiatrists, psychologists, social workers, nurses, and occupational therapists—would use their various techniques to assess each person's difficulties. For some people, there seemed to be no problems apparent on the surface of their lives that could explain their depression. They did not seem to have any financial worries. They did not seem to be going through any relationship breakdowns or suffering from any physical ailments. They were not experiencing major disruptions at work. Everything seemed to be in order. This baffled and confused us all. There seemed to be no legitimate explanation for the depression these patients experienced. As I look back, I think it would be safe to state that these patients were in the later stages of the blues. They had drifted along without paying attention to their extreme demands regarding work, family, and life in general. Because their exaggerated expectations were not being satisfied, these people burned out. Only when things got really bad, and they were feeling extremely depressed, did they finally realize that they needed help from our mental health services.

It is important to know, however, that being burned out does not necessarily mean that you are burned up. Even if you are in the later stages of burnout, you are not necessarily destined to stay there. Strategies to deal with burnout will be detailed in Chapter 7.

6 There Are No Hopeless Situations, Only People Who Think Hopelessly

Twelve Myths About the Blues

Victims of the blues usually have very active imaginations. To explain away their woes and sorrows, they may blame the workplace, colleagues, managers, the company, friends, relatives, and situations. It is as if the workplace has done them in, and that is why they are "out of it." But the blues are rarely that simple. It is perfectly true that severe changes in the workplace can be associated with feeling down. But to go one step further and say that the workplace causes all of one's problems doesn't make sense. The blues stem from extreme demands and expectations. These do not originate in the workplace and they are not created by colleagues and managers—or anyone else, for that matter.

An athlete whom I counseled had a real knack for blaming everyone but himself for a slump he was experiencing. This consequently hurt him much worse in the end.

I knew that I was in a slump, but everyone was always on my case! My coach and manager always asked me how I was doing. They urged me to take extra practice to sharpen my skills. Why didn't they leave me alone? If I wanted extra practice, I'd take it! They didn't have to remind me. Then there was my wife. She would always ask how I was feeling. She knew I was in a slump, so how should I feel? Then the other players wanted to work out with me. Why all of a sudden was I getting all this attention? If people just laid off me, I probably would have gotten out of the slump. But I didn't. So I began to hate people and blamed them even more for my mess. Then one day the manager told me that I had a real attitude problem. It just went from bad to worse!

Blues victims have a strong tendency to come up with explanations for their problems that I refer to as "myths." This chapter seeks to dispel these myths and points out how insufficient they are when cited as causes of the blues. This is not to say that these myths are not significant. But more significant are the cravings and demands underpinning the myths.

The thinking behind these myths may resemble the unreasonable ideas described in the discussion on pressure. But myths about the blues are cynical and pessimistic, whereas the unreasonable ideas are worried, fretful, and fearful in nature. Also keep in mind that these myths lead to withdrawal, isolation, and resignation, whereas the unreasonable thoughts result in indecision, avoidance, and aggression.

1. Work Overload

The phenomenon of work overload may be very real. Some people have tremendous amounts of work to do. But to say that work overload is the sole cause of the blues is at least questionable.

Blues victims typically make a number of unique demands that relate to their work overload. Unless they examine these exaggerated beliefs, they will never deal adequately with their unhappiness. Furthermore, they will not be able to deal with the problem, if it is a problem, of having too much work to do.

Blues victims tend to reason along the following lines: "There is too much to do, but I have to do it all, and I have to do it perfectly." They feel that they should be able to handle everything. They need to be in control. If they are not in control, then they think: "The heck with everything."

2. Work Underload

Work underload may also be a real phenomenon. Some people believe that not having enough work on their plates is a sure sign that they must be failing, that people do not trust them enough, and that they are not going to get anywhere in the organization. But whether work underload is a real concern or not, examining the exaggerated expectations that underlie this particular complaint is important. What are the unreasonable beliefs that lie behind this myth? They go as follows: "I have to have more work; otherwise I am a failure." Or: "I should be more productive, more useful, more fully occupied. Because I am not, I will never be able to make progress within the company." Not only do these notions require examination; they also need to be changed.

3. ROLE AMBIGUITY

Some blues victims complain that they really don't know what they are supposed to be doing on the job. Because they are so confused, they get very discouraged. Role ambiguity may in fact be a problem, but whether it is doesn't really matter, at least initially. First, identify the extreme demands; then pay attention to the other details. The exaggerated beliefs that lie behind this myth may go as follows: "I need my job and I should be treated well. Because I am not being treated with consideration, the heck with it!" Or "I cannot stand the uncertainty. I cannot stand the confusion about what my job is supposed to consist of. Because I cannot be totally efficient, I will never amount to anything." By subscribing to these deeply rooted beliefs, blues candidates set themselves up for major headaches.

4. INADEQUATE RESOURCES

Blues victims sometimes believe their dilemmas are caused by a lack of resources with which to perform their jobs. Again, it may be true that there are insufficient personnel to perform all the necessary tasks and activities; the division or department may not have adequate resources. But whether or not resources are an issue, what is really giving grief to the blues victims are the extreme beliefs that underlie this particular myth. These beliefs may include: "They have no right to give me inadequate help. How will I ever get on the fast track?" Or "I always have to do everything on my own. I always have to be responsible for everything. I can't stand it anymore."

These notions are the real villains! If work overload, work underload, role ambiguity, or inadequate resources truly caused the blues, then every person who experienced these particular conditions would be suffering. But they are not. Some people encounter these conditions yet are not bothered. The people who are down are those who hold rigid and uncompromising beliefs about how the workplace should be. And when things don't work out as they should, these same people degrade and debase themselves and the people around them.

5. Uncooperative Colleagues

Some blues victims subscribe to the myth that their problems are caused by uncooperative colleagues. They may claim: "It's those yo-yos, those turkeys, those misfits with whom I have to work who are ultimately causing my burnout!" Or: "If I were removed from this department or work group, everything would be okay." You may be working with uncooperative colleagues, or you may not, but they are not the cause of your woes. The critical element once again is those improbable beliefs. It is the presumption that other people have no right to be uncooperative—that you are a better person than they are—that causes the problems. It is the belief that other people will prevent you from achieving success that leads to the blues.

Let us assume that you are working with uncooperative colleagues. Will these particular expectations and attitudes help you to get along? Of course not. They will produce anger and animosity. Will your anger and aggression make it easier for you to work with them as a team? Not a chance!

Let me digress briefly. In the 1970s, we were told that the best way to deal with anger and aggression was to get it out. We were advised to release all our inner hostility. Once it was discharged, we were assured that we would feel a lot better and would ultimately be a lot healthier. The trend has continued into the 1980s, 1990s, and 2000s. People let their emotions erupt all over the place. Just drive the busy morning rush hour and you'll see a variety of emotions displayed.

We have been very innovative in finding ways to express our anger. For example, we have bought big stuffed toys called "Bobo dolls," taken them down to the basement, stuck a picture of the person we hate most (be it a colleague or supervisor) on the head of the doll, and began to punch it. Some of us have simply hung up a punching bag in our basement and pounded the heck out of it. We have purchased "aggression bats," sponge bats intended to be used to hit (painlessly) people with whom you felt extremely angry. Can you picture actually walloping a colleague with your aggression bat? In Japan, some companies have constructed padded rooms. Employees are encouraged to enter these rooms before the workday starts. They are supposed to relieve themselves of all their pent-up emotions by screaming, punching, and kicking. It is assumed that they will then be better able to deal with their fellow employees and handle their work more effectively.

It is an interesting commentary on the human condition that we resort to all these ridiculous activities in order to get rid of our anger. We are finding out, however, that these activities do not have the desired effect. If you engage in these zany tactics, the only probable result is that you will become an expert at being angry. If you practice any behavior over and over again, you become skilled at it. Imagine being a master of aggression! The danger is that one day you may forget to punch a bag and instead punch a human being. You might end up swatting a colleague or smacking your supervisor. In fact, violence in the workplace has escalated! This surely is not behavior that is likely to secure advancement for the perpetrator.

Before you express your anger and blame the world for your misery, think. What is going on inside your head that is getting you so worked up? What extreme beliefs are putting you in this position? Once you figure this out and change it, you are more likely to behave in a constructive fashion.

6. LACK OF FEEDBACK

Lack of feedback may or may not be a real issue, but it is not the cause of blues. It is important to identify the unusual beliefs that give rise to the blues. These may go as follows: "No one cares about what I do; I must not be worth anything, and I'll never succeed." Or "I need to be recognized. I need to be told that I am worthwhile. Because no one tells me this, it must mean that I am failing miserably." It is these pessimistic ideas that create the problems.

7. Too Much Supervision

Blues victims may also ascribe their misfortune to too-close supervision. At the root of this myth is the belief that they are supervised closely because they aren't trusted. They feel that they are being treated like children and consequently will never get anywhere.

I do not mean to minimize the importance of what goes on in any given organization. Certainly, there are predicaments, events, and situations that are troublesome. I am, however, concerned about people who always demand that the organization do something or that the company remedy this or change that. When the changes are not forthcoming, these people become very negative and cynical about themselves and the world around them. I am concerned about people who do not take charge of their own health and well-being. Once they have solved their own problems, then they can attempt to change things in the organization. The people who burn out are the ones who get stuck and never get unstuck. They believe that the company has an obligation to eliminate all the wrongs in the workplace, so that they feel better, healthier, and more productive. It is this attitude that concerns me!

I counseled a high-school teacher who was convinced that her school should change so that her needs would be properly satisfied. Not only did the school fail to change, but other teachers began to see her as a problem:

> As a teacher, I have always devoted myself to being the best that I can be. And I guess I expected the same from the school I work at. So I found that after a while I couldn't tolerate the inconsistencies and the mess our department was in. First of all, I had too much work to do. My classrooms were overloaded with students, my responsibilities as assistant head were very unclear, and my department head didn't really trust me. I got so fed up that I demanded that the school and the principal do something. I demanded that corrective action be taken immediately. I went on like this for months. Eventually, I found out that my colleagues saw me as having a chip on my shoulder and as a troublemaker. But I was serious. And my health was also beginning to suffer. I couldn't eat properly. I couldn't sleep properly. And my friends didn't want to be with me. But worst of all, my teaching was slipping. One day, a close colleague took me aside. She literally shook me. She told me that I can't always have what I want, when I want it. The hardest thing for me to realize was that the system didn't have to change just because I demanded that it should. Although there are very real problems in our department, it takes patience and negotiation to bring about change.

8. OUT-OF-DATE PROCEDURES

Another myth that victims often believe is that the blues are caused by outdated policies and procedures. Again, this condition may or may not exist. But examine the underlying expectations first. The victims may say, for example: "Why do I always have to put up with stupid policies? I am always the one who has to do things perfectly. I simply can't stand this anymore. I will never achieve excellence this way."

9. LACK OF STIMULATION

Some people believe that their blues are caused by lack of stimulation and job enrichment. This myth is very significant. Certain people are notorious for demanding that their jobs be exciting, enriching, and stimulating each and every day of their lives. Underlying this demand is the belief that there is nothing interesting outside of work. And if work is not totally and completely enriching, then the victim is doomed to a life of mediocrity.

10. LACK OF RECOGNITION

Another myth: the blues are caused by lack of reward and recognition for good work. The underlying belief in this case is that the individual needs to feel that she is good. Indeed, she needs to feel that she is great, that she is doing a fantastic job. If she is not getting recognition for doing a great job, it must mean that she is failing.

11. JOB RELOCATION

A myth that has recently become prominent is that the blues are caused by job relocation. Some employees are asked to take a number of job transfers during the course of their careers. Some do it willingly; others are simply not prepared to move. Specific consequences may be attached to their decisions. People who refuse to move may not climb the corporate ladder as quickly.

They may not always receive rewarding projects to work on. But, essentially, they accept the consequences of their decisions.

There are other people who do transfer but blame the relocation for their burnout. If you decided to relocate because of the possible advantages of doing so yet blame all your woes and miseries on the transfer, then there is something grossly wrong. Before you start to fault the organization and the relocation for your problems, examine your own beliefs. They might include: "I need stability in my life. How dare they do this to me!" Or "I have to have my roots; it is impossible to go on like this!" If stability and permanence are important to you, why did you make the move in the first place? Presumably you did so in the expectation that certain career advantages would follow. You want to have your cake and eat it too. But because of your unreasonable beliefs, not only will you be miserable but you will also be unable to enjoy the benefits of relocation.

12. JOB INSECURITY

The final myth is that the blues are caused by downsizing and job insecurity. This is a very real situation in a number or organizations. Certain companies are undoubtedly going through staff reductions. Some of the survivors may, in fact, feel quite vulnerable. The beliefs that make the situation especially upsetting for blues candidates are: "I need security. I need to know exactly what is going on with my career, otherwise I will never get ahead. I need to be able to plan for the future, otherwise the present is meaningless." These beliefs are killers! No person today has an absolute guarantee of job security. I am not downplaying the importance of staff reductions and their impact on the people who are left behind. But you have a choice. You can upset yourself a great deal, or you can learn to deal more effectively with change.

I hope that you now understand and recognize that the blues are chiefly brought on by exaggerated and extreme expectations and beliefs, accompanied by cynical, pessimistic thinking. That is not to downplay the effects of real organizational conditions and situations. But we cannot necessarily blame our feelings or our blues symptoms on what the organization is doing to us. We first need to clarify our own expectations and examine what we are saying to ourselves. We need to determine whether we are too demanding and too negative. Once we have done that, it is possible to look at the company and figure out what problems we wish to address. We'll accomplish far more with this approach!

The Blues and Male Menopause

Many men have recently decided that the explanation of their blues is "male menopause." This, for some men, is an extremely convenient explanation because it seems to simplify their problems and absolve them of all responsibility. However, male menopause is a big myth. Not only does it not account for a man's difficulties, it does not exist.

Supposedly, when a man reaches his forties or fifties, strange biological drives, urges, and irregularities occur. He may run into certain emotional problems. He may find himself very unhappy at work, at home or in his relationships. Consequently, he may be driven to do unusual things. He may suddenly quit his job in favor of an activity that is more artistic and spirited in nature. He may take up carpentry, farming, or painting. He may become an acolyte of Hare Krishna, join the Moonies, or study yoga. Or he may decide to have an affair, often with a woman fifteen or twenty years his junior.

The beauty of this supposed syndrome is that it gives a man an easy way out. In essence, he is no longer answerable for his actions. He can simply say that because he is experiencing male menopause, you have to accept him the way he is. He can do as he pleases. This is utter nonsense!

To blame the blues on male menopause is another major copout. In using this myth as an excuse, a man says to his company that he is not accountable for what he is feeling, thinking, or doing. Nor is he responsible for the changes that need to be made to correct matters. If he's doing unsatisfactory work there is nothing he can do about it. He is being biologically driven to carry on this way. Matters may eventually correct themselves, but those in the workplace and at home will have to be patient and wait.

This line of reasoning and this abdication of responsibility are really part of the blues syndrome. In fact, if you use male

menopause to explain away your problems, you are simply rein-
forcing your blues. You are permitting the symptoms to continue. With the passage of time, the symptoms will either stay
the same or, more likely, get worse.

It is important to understand that menopause in men is not
a physiological condition as it is in women. There are no unusual
drives or urges that occur in the male when he enters his forties or
fifties. In essence, the myth of male menopause involves an abundance of exaggerated expectations that have been unfulfilled. It
is the accumulation of one's frustrations, irritations, annoyances,
and anger with the workplace and the world. It entails disen-
chantment with yourself and the people around you.

The Blues and the Midlife Crisis

As human beings, we'll resort to any explanation that will excuse
us from being responsible for our blues. "Midlife crisis" is probably the single most popular label used to account for the miseries
of the world. It is more common than male menopause because
it affects both men and women. This phenomenon supposedly
occurs during the mid-forties. It is that moment of truth, that cli-
max, when we come to grips with who we are, what we have and
have not accomplished, what we have done with our careers and
our families, and the fact that we are vulnerable and destructible.
Certain people are so unhappy with what they discover that they
stay in a crisis indefinitely.

People who are unhappy at work, who are desperately struggling and are burned out are sometimes quick to blame midlife crisis for their condition. They are often convinced that their midlife crisis will escalate until they fall apart and have a nervous breakdown. They are convinced that they will never recover from their breakdown and will probably remain vegetables for the rest of their careers.

I hate to disappoint you, but there really is no midlife crisis. Like male menopause, this so-called syndrome is not a special condition that suddenly appears just because we reach our mid-forties. We can experience crises at any time during our lives. Some people regularly question what they've accomplished and the direction their careers are taking. Such self-examinations are not confined to midlife, although some people do wait until then to take a good, hard look at themselves.

The worst part of this midlife phenomenon is that people use it to absolve themselves of the responsibility for their troubles. This is silly. We are responsible for our problems. What is noteworthy is that this so-called crisis—like many of our troubles that may take place in our twenties, thirties, and forties—is connected to those extreme beliefs and expectations that we have buried away in our heads. Therefore, let's stop looking for a convenient scapegoat, such as male menopause or midlife crisis, to explain away our blues. Instead, let us focus our energies and attention on those treacherous and misguided ideas in our minds that do wreak havoc in our lives.

7 Practical Strategies for Combatting the Blues

Cooling Your Jets

All of us have the ability to remove ourselves from a situation and cool off. You have probably done this frequently, or at least on occasion, perhaps without really paying attention to it. For example, say you are involved in a heated debate with a colleague or friend. Rather than continue this debate, which may end up in a serious argument, you say to the other person: "Why don't we cool off for a while and come back to this later?" You simply remove yourself from the situation.

Another example: You may step back and cool off before you buy something extravagant. Say that you drop into a local art gallery and you suddenly come across a painting that knocks your socks off. You can just see it hanging in your favorite room at home. You look at the price tag and are confronted with a figure of $10,000. Before pulling out your checkbook, you say to yourself: "Wait a minute. Maybe I should look around some other galleries." In essence, you have stepped back, detached yourself from the situation, and reconsidered the matter. It does not mean that you will not buy this particular piece of art. It simply means that you have decided to think about it and determine whether you truly wish to purchase this piece.

Or maybe one evening you are trying to be the model parent, but your child is not cooperating. He has decided to throw a temper tantrum and is screaming, yelling, kicking the floor, and threatening to throw up. Rather than "smack" him, you decide to step back and cool off. You go into your bedroom and get away from it all. This is, in effect, a time-out procedure. Once you have settled down and reconsidered the situation, you can return and deal with your child in a more composed and even-tempered manner.

So, cooling off basically means that you step back and distance yourself from the problem in order to reexamine your options. It is difficult to think clearly in the midst of chaos or conflict; this method affords you the opportunity.

I recall talking to a real estate executive who had an intriguing way of distancing herself and cooling off:

> When, occasionally, I got into a serious debate with a client or colleague, I would remove myself from the exchange by stating that I wanted to think about things for a short time and that I would get back to the individual soon. Then I locked myself away in a quiet room, usually my office. Sitting down, I would close my eyes and imagine myself as a third party, watching these two people engaged in

a heated exchange. As an onlooker, I tried to figure out what I would do to improve matters so that the disagreement could be resolved. As soon as I was able to come up with a reasonable solution, I opened my eyes and called up the other person. I'm not saying that this technique is easy. But with practice, I was able to master it. Ultimately, I could get away from any heated debate. I especially tried to remove myself from those disagreements which might possibly lose business for me.

Mirror, Mirror on the Wall

A very important strategy when it comes to the blues is self-awareness, or self-assessment. It is useful to determine just how upset and distraught you really are. In essence, this means sitting down and taking an inventory of your thoughts and feelings and figuring out how much you are really suffering. This assessment can be done with a series of questions. If most of the answers suggest that your career and life in general are not too satisfying, then you can assume that you are suffering from the blues and may be on your way to depression.

YOUR BLUES QUOTIENT

Rate yourself on how you react to each of the questions posed below. Then total up your score and read the appropriate description.

4 = Always 3 = Frequently 2 = Sometimes 1 = Never

_____Has work lost its appeal and attraction?

_____Is work draining?

_____Do you find your energy sapped after work?

_____Are you no longer enthusiastic about your work?

_____Are you cynical about the way you are being treated at work?

_____Are you preoccupied with what would happen to you if you lost your job?

_____Does your job seem meaningless to you right now?

_____Do you force yourself to do routine things at work?

_____Do your colleagues, even management, goof off all the time and not pull their own weight?

_____Is your department, your division, or your entire organization a maze of red tape and foul-ups?

_____Do you constantly want to be somewhere else rather than at work?

_____Do you find that you no longer enjoy being with friends and colleagues?

_____Do you feel yourself drifting away from your family and relatives?

_____Do you look for more-dangerous diversions and activities to bring excitement into your life?

_____Do you feel resigned rather than enthusiastic about your future?

_____**TOTAL**

SCORE

15–30 You struggle at times with your job and those you work with.

31–45 Your level of the blues is reaching risky proportions.

46–60 You have a high level of cynicism, defeatism, and
negativity; if it persists, you may find yourself
depressed, if you are not already so.

These scores and descriptions are not designed to label you or
scare you but to draw your attention to what is going on. It is
critical to be aware of your thoughts and feelings. Awareness
precedes the motivation to change. The more you realize how
unhappy and unfulfilled you are, the more you may be inspired
to make some changes in your life.

Ten Steps to Debunking

Distorted beliefs and exaggerated expectations are the most critical ingredients regarding the blues. Changing those beliefs is fundamental if the blues are to be thwarted. By changing distorted
beliefs, I mean reducing their intensity and diminishing their
extreme and demanding properties so that they become more sensible. This does not necessarily mean that you give up your beliefs
and expectations. It means that you transform them into ones that
are more realistic. Once you do this, you will begin to establish a
"detached concern" that finally has limits. Being involved in and
committed to your job and the work you do will still be important
to you, but this commitment will go only so far.

Such limits are valuable because if you are too consumed
by extreme demands you don't perform as well. I'm sure that

we have all seen instances in which someone has tried so hard to achieve a particular result that the exact opposite happened. Athletes are notorious for this. Some become so concerned about getting a hit, scoring a goal, catching a pass, or sinking a putt that they blow it. Most athletes eventually learn that they cannot afford to take things too seriously or be too demanding; otherwise their performance suffers rather than improves. They learn to try their best, nothing more.

It is important for us to develop the same frame of mind. To do this, you need to alter your beliefs and expectations to minimize their demanding properties. This will allow you to gain control over and reverse the process of the blues and ultimate depression. Following are 10 steps that will help you debunk the myths and get you on the right track.

1. OPEN ADMISSION

A critical first step is to admit that you are suffering from the blues. This sounds like a very simple matter, but it is not. Many victims will not reveal their problems to anyone. Certain people will not take on the responsibility of even conceding to themselves, let alone others, that they are in fact suffering from the blues or depression. In making the admission, you clearly demonstrate to yourself and to the key people in your workplace or life that you are experiencing problems. When you have stopped fighting the fact that you are suffering, you can start to do something about it.

Alcoholism is another example in which open admission of the problem is necessary to the rehabilitation process. One of the most important steps to recovery is for an alcoholic to admit that he or she is an alcoholic. This is one of the guiding rules of Alcoholics Anonymous (AA). AA makes it clear to its members that it is very, very important to announce to yourself and the people around you that you are, in fact, an alcoholic. Once you have accomplished this, you are on the road to recovery.

Yet another example relates to those who are overweight. If you have ever been involved in a structured weight-loss program, you will know that one of the first steps to losing weight is to admit that you are overweight. If you deny the fact that you have a weight problem, then you are not motivated to do anything about it. Only if your motivation is strong will you be able to lose weight.

Admitting their problems works for alcoholics and for people who are attempting to lose weight, and it can also work for blues victims. It will work because you are no longer running away from the problem; you are prepared to face it head-on.

2. Taking Responsibility

The next step is to declare that you created the problem. Blues victims, as we have seen, are notorious for blaming everybody around them for their troubles. They are the first to state that their colleagues, management, and the company messed up their careers and made them miserable. If you adopt this perspective, you will have to wait until "they" decide to make things better for you. If "they" don't make things better, you're out of luck. Doesn't it make more sense to acknowledge that you created the blues problem? Then the onus is on you to do something about it.

You can manage your difficulties. Why leave it in the hands of someone else? The one thing that most blues victims fear is loss of control. As they burn out, they convince themselves that they are losing the power to run their own lives. That power is never lost; in fact, it is used to develop unreasonable beliefs and expectations. Instead, you can use this control to develop more sensible ideas. It is very exciting to know that you can do something about your own difficulties. You can take charge of the direction that your career will take. You can be the person responsible for changing things so that the blues no longer play a role in your life.

3. SELF-ACCEPTANCE

Do not condemn yourself for being blue. Blues victims are notoriously hard on themselves. By condemning yourself, you simply escalate your symptoms. Why magnify your problem? Accept the fact that you are troubled and go on from there. Being self-critical serves no useful purpose. Besides, if you are depressed, will thinking negative and cynical thoughts make it easier for you? Are you looking for a life of constant self-criticism? You can stop it. And it is important to stop it, because if you are caught up in feeling sorry for yourself, you may have no energy, vitality, or effort left for constructive change.

Incidentally, discomfort, hurt, and pain are part and parcel of feeling blue. They are also part of the process of change. Blues victims are convinced that once they start to feel pain and emotional hurt, these feelings will escalate; they will be psychologically ripped apart and will never recover. Pain is certainly unpleasant, but it does not signal the end of the world. If the blues victim is convinced that hurt is equivalent to ruination, he will probably be deterred from striving to change his life. So it is important to realize that we are not so fragile, that we will not burst at the seams as we make adjustments in our lives. Remember the expression, "There is no gain without (at least a little) pain."

4. CHALLENGE

It is important that blues victims challenge their low frustration tolerance. Blues victims are notorious for believing that they cannot tolerate anything. They wake up in the morning and say that they cannot endure getting out of bed, putting their clothes on, having to rush out of the house, or driving to work. They cannot face their colleagues. They cannot stomach dealing with management. They cannot endure having to go to meetings. They cannot tolerate having to face deadlines. They cannot swallow having to answer the phone. They are at their lowest point of tolerance. They are about to crack and may even have a nervous breakdown.

In fact, there is no such thing as a "nervous breakdown." Nerves don't just break down! People can certainly give up the will to carry on, but nerves do not come apart and stop working.

Human beings are fairly resilient. We can tolerate quite a bit of frustration. We all know of people who have gone through very serious changes, traumas, or crises in their lives and have still managed to endure. We know of colleagues, friends, and relatives who have been through a variety of "pressure cookers" in their careers and were able to tolerate the frustration and disappointment that occurred. We can probably think of experiences we ourselves have been through and have withstood reasonably well. Therefore, even if you are feeling blue, you don't have to give up. It is important to remind yourself regularly that you can endure far more than you give yourself credit for.

5. A New Philosophy

It is important that blues victims change their philosophical approach and adopt a philosophy of uncertainty. Blues victims crave certainty. They want to know for certain that things will get better. They want to know for certain that they will be successful again. They want to be reassured that they will overcome their issues. They want to know for sure that they will be valued again by their colleagues and managers. They want a lot of guarantees.

But what do we know for certain? What can we really predict? We are surrounded by many changes each and every day. How can we demand that events occur in a specific way, at a specific time? Is it sensible to be upset when events don't unfold just the way we believe they should? But some people do this to themselves. When their demands are frustrated, they are ready to predict the end of their careers. Giving up this notion makes living a lot easier.

6. REDUCTION OF NEEDS

It is important for blues victims to dedicate themselves to reducing their necessities and conditions for living. We know that blues victims have a long list of requirements: two cars, designer clothing, a big house, a laptop, a Palm Pilot, and so on. They have to have an excellent job, make a fantastic salary, occupy a phenomenal office. The list of necessities goes on and on. If these were necessary conditions to sustain life on this earth, the world would have few survivors. In fact, many people go into work every day to an environment that is not ideal by any stretch of the imagination. They might not have the biggest office or make the most money. They might not regularly get promotions. They might not have the latest toys. Yet they maintain a good level of productivity, are reasonably content, and retain a sense of humor.

I would like to emphasize again that I am not suggesting that you shy away from putting your best foot forward. But if your list of necessary conditions is too long, you are causing yourself a great deal of hardship and pressure, and the blues are just around the corner. In order to lessen your turmoil, try to realize that what you demand might be better stated in terms of what you "prefer" or "would like." You can certainly strive for what you prefer. But if you make a demand and your demand is not satisfied, then you are demoralizing yourself. Continue to put out your best effort. Perform to your capabilities. Perhaps you will get most of what you would like to get, but there are no guarantees.

Sooner or later, blues victims must come to the realization that their conditions for living are not really essential at all. They are simply one definition of what life could be. If you define your life according to a variety of extreme beliefs and exaggerated expectations, you will experience resentment, bitterness, hardship, and possible depression. On the other hand, if your ideas are not extreme and exaggerated, you can roll with the punches. Many a successful executive has stated that people who do well are not those who handle the ups in their careers but those who manage the downs.

As part of the reduction of needs, blues victims would be wise to consider eliminating their tremendous need for success. This notion may be quite controversial. Blues victims maintain that their lives must be filled with prosperity, accomplishment, and attainment. For them, success and achievement are as necessary to survival as food and drink. But if you approach accomplishment and good fortune in this way, you are asking for trouble. Should you not satisfy these so-called "basic needs," you would "die" psychologically, just as you would die physically without food and drink. No wonder blues victims have trouble turning themselves around and get depressed! Their views of success and achievement are completely and grossly distorted.

Another very important corollary to this idea is to get rid of the notion that only job success gives meaning to your life. Blues victims are wholeheartedly committed to achieving success at all costs. Even in the latter stages of burnout, they continue to beat themselves into the ground. They believe that if they can just get that one shred of job success, they can turn their careers around. It is almost as if triumph on the job is the only thing that keeps them going. Isn't this a bit extreme? Why should job success be the only thing that gives meaning to life? We as human beings can be fulfilled in many ways. We can enjoy our familial relationships. We can derive satisfaction from our social relationships. We can gain joy from our spiritual involvements. We can derive happiness from religious observance. We can obtain pleasure from our leisure activities. We can follow through on a variety of pursuits that are very gratifying.

What is very interesting is that if we gain considerable fulfillment from our outside activities, we end up doing better on the job because we come to work in a much better state of mind—not demanding that we be successful but with the intention of doing the best we can. If we are not as impressive as we would like to be today, we say to ourselves that there is always tomorrow. The fewer demands we place on our work and careers, the less pressure we feel and the less frustration we encounter. Therefore, we end up performing far more satisfactorily. If you give up the notion that only job success gives meaning to your life, then you will probably experience greater job success. Isn't this motivation enough to change your exaggerated expectations?

7. REJECT PERFECTIONISM

It is important to be anti-perfectionistic. This injunction might truly exasperate blues victims, who dedicate their lives to perfection! Typically, they believe that if they try a little bit harder to produce that perfect project, to write that perfect proposal, to give that perfect presentation, then, and only then, will their depressive symptoms disappear. It is as if the solution to all of their problems is to be infallible. After all, society values perfection; families value perfection. What other answer is there to their misery but the glorious pursuit of precision and exactitude?

However, researchers and health practitioners have found that if you dedicate yourself to perfection, you will achieve the exact opposite. Isn't that a crazy contradiction? If you are compelled to pursue that incomparable state of exactitude, you will probably not succeed because none of us knows what perfection truly is. What is ideal for one person may not be ideal for another. What may excite a colleague may not turn on your manager. Perhaps your manager's definition of perfection should be yours. But what if you do not agree with your manager's definition? What if your manager is replaced by another manager? What if your manager changes her mind about what is and is not perfect? Do you see how silly the whole notion of perfectionism really is?

So why not convince yourself that perfectionism is not worth pursuing? Instead, believe that you will do your best. And if your best is not good enough, at least you have tried. If you are able to consistently maintain this attitude, you will find that you are less disturbed, less agitated, and more productive.

8. JUDGMENT

Another very important consideration is to make certain not to judge yourself. Blues victims routinely evaluate themselves. Indeed, they go one step further: they judge themselves very harshly. If you debase yourself, if you degrade yourself, we now know that you will probably end up feeling depressed.

Depression occurs among those who specialize in self-deprecation. Blues victims do not leave themselves alone! They are critical of how they perform on the job, of how they act at home, of how they relate in social situations. They are critical of how they do everything in life. They end up despising themselves to the point where they do not even want to be with themselves.

Does that make sense? Is it helpful in any way? Will it allow you to deal with your problems effectively? Blues victims truly believe that, because they have done poorly, they must be no good. Because their performance is inadequate, they must be inept and unfit. So they continue to berate themselves and end up feeling rotten in the process.

The answer is to not judge yourself. If you must judge anything, then rate your actions. If you have done something well at work, you can say to yourself: "That project turned out fine. I shall still strive for continued excellence in my work." If your performance was not so satisfactory, you can say to yourself: "That did not go well. I will make an effort to improve my work in the future." But to reason that because your performance was inadequate you are inadequate will lead to one big headache. You'll hate yourself and hate your work. Focus your attention on what you are doing. Try to correct your performance. Leave yourself out of it. A blues victim might say: "I am my performance. If my performance is rotten, that means I am rotten." This is nonsense. If you have not done well at a particular task, it has no general implications for you as a human being.

A corollary to this principle is to ensure that you do not attach your ego or your identity to your achievements. If your ego is associated with your accomplishments, and your achievements don't materialize the way you demand, then what are you left with? Basically you are left with a shattered ego. If you separate your identity from your achievements, you can examine these accomplishments objectively. You can assess what you have and have not done well. You can then focus your attention on how to correct your failures and meet your objectives. When you allow your ego to enter into all your activities, you can drive yourself to distraction. Then you can focus your energy and attention on yourself rather than on your work.

Once you accept that you are who you are regardless of your successes or failures, you have made a major step forward. You will then be able to deal with criticism, rejection, and failure. If you spend time worrying about yourself and your ego, how will you ever change? Blues victims don't have an answer to that question. Rejoice in the opportunity to disassociate yourself from what you do! Enjoy your achievements! Correct your failures! Then, and only then, will you get more out of your career and out of life. You will certainly find work more rewarding and the workplace more stimulating.

A further corollary to this principle is that you strive to accept yourself without any conditions or prerequisites. Blues victims are constantly comparing themselves to others. They might laugh at this and say: "Isn't that just like a psychologist?! You should never accept yourself, because if you do you will never succeed. You will never have any motivation or drive. You will settle for mediocrity and never go beyond that." I'll tell you something interesting. If you can truly accept yourself as you are, think of the energy, drive, and inspiration that will be freed up for what you want in your career. You will no longer be bound by who you should be like, how you should talk, how you should act, and how you should perform.

Let me draw an analogy to one of mankind's major concerns: losing weight. Most people are obsessed with their figures and their weight. Certain people seem to lose weight more easily than others. These people do not allow their egos or their pride to get entangled with their weight loss. They recognize that they need to shed some pounds, focus their attention on their performance, and proceed in a disciplined fashion to reach their target. But other people let their egos get involved with their weight-loss programs. These people struggle because they cannot accept themselves. They blame themselves for their rotten looks. They compare themselves to skinny people. They hate the way they look, the way they walk, the way they dress. If you think this way, you will certainly not be motivated to lose weight. If attention is always directed at *you,* it will be next to impossible to concentrate on what you need to do to lose weight. But if you accept yourself, though not necessarily accept what you do with food, all your energy and attention can be focused on the weight loss. Typically, people who can do that also do much better at shedding the pounds. This example points out why it is so important to accept yourself. Once you do, you can then get on with the task at hand, unhindered by your ego.

It is equally important that you accept others and their idiosyncrasies. Blues victims find this extremely difficult. They storm around criticizing not only themselves but especially others. They blame others for their personal failures. They condemn others for their own insecurities. They blame their colleagues, management, and family for all their defeats. What will continuing in this way really achieve? It certainly will not help you in your daily working relationships. If blues victims did not have such high expectations of others, they would probably not malign and denounce people so much. But why do you need to demand so much of others? Why should you expect others to be what you want them to be? Would it not be easier to accept others and their temperaments, idiosyncrasies, and mannerisms? A blues victim might reply: "This is typical of a psychologist. He is telling us to love everybody. He is telling us to keep our mouths shut and to walk about with big smiles on our faces, as if everything were just perfect and wonderful."

To allow people their personal styles, their idiosyncrasies, and their dispositions does not necessarily mean that you cannot challenge what they say and do. But challenging people's behavior is not the same as rejecting or disliking them. If you hate a person, you usually have nothing to do with him or her, or you fight a lot. The reason you conduct yourself in this destructive fashion is that you expect others to change because you want them to be different, to do what you want them to do. Wouldn't it be wiser to accept them as they are? They are their own unique selves. Don't pay attention to their egos or personalities; simply focus on how they behave. If you disagree with their behavior, you can challenge it. Wouldn't you then find work more enjoyable? You might even have a good time working with your colleagues and management. You might even enjoy your family more and ultimately control your blues problem more effectively.

I can hear the blues victims saying: "Okay, how will I be competitive? If I accept people and am nice to them, I will end up being a wimp! People will push me around. I will not be tough anymore, and I won't be as successful." This is ridiculous! If you accept others, your energies are freed up to work with people more effectively and even to compete more effectively.

Let me give you an example. Say a colleague is critical of some of the work you have done. If you have always demanded, in a rigid and uncompromising fashion, that your colleagues respect everything you do, then you would be extremely upset. You would be angry. You would probably not want to have anything to do with her. However, if you accept the fact that she has the right to be critical if she chooses, it would make work easier for you. It would allow you to focus your attention on the criticisms being offered. You would then be able to figure out whether they were legitimate. If the criticisms were legitimate, you could make the necessary changes. You might even go further and come up with improvements. Being able to effectively solve problems and remain innovative in the process would place you in a highly enviable position. You might now be viewed as a person who can handle criticism and devise solutions even "under fire," someone who could compete with the best of them. All this could come about because you allowed yourself to accept others, thereby focusing on the criticisms and their legitimacy.

Why do you think office politics is so rampant? It is widespread because employees do not accept one another. What if you changed your outlook? What if you said to yourself, "Okay, people can dress the way they want. People can say and do what they choose to. If what they say and do is not appropriate, I can challenge their actions if I choose to." With these views, do you still think that you would hate your fellow workers? Do you think that you would fight with them as much? Avoid them as much? I believe the answer is an emphatic "no"!

The key is to separate people from what they say and do. People are who they are. You are who you are. People do not have to be the way you demand. Colleagues, supervisors, managers, family, and friends, for that matter, do not have to conform to your expectations. When a controversial situation comes up and you are troubled by it, don't despise the person it's coming from. Animosity, antagonism, and bitterness are a tremendous waste of energy and spirit. Such conflict can destroy a department or even a whole organization, and certainly a family. It guarantees that teamwork is out the window. Enjoy the human differences in this world. Accept that people are their unique selves. Challenge differences in approach or basic objectives and try to work them out. But keep your ego, and the egos of your colleagues, out of it.

9. INSPIRATION

Another significant realization is that you don't necessarily need motivation and inspiration to do your job. Furthermore, you don't have to enjoy something in order to do it. Blues victims, however, are committed to the mistaken belief that they need to be roused, moved, and invigorated each and every working day. They need to feel gratification and excitement from everything they are involved in; otherwise they simply cannot perform. Is this really true? Do we have to feel this way in order to perform? Of course not. We all know of many instances where others were not totally inspired by or overjoyed about a particular task, but they still did it. Is it reasonable and realistic to demand that you be exhilarated each and every day? Blues victims demand this of themselves. They also demand that the workplace bristle with stimulants. No wonder they find it difficult to do their jobs! They're spending too much time in their vivid fantasy lives, dreaming about how things should be.

You might ask, "What if I am never inspired or motivated, or I never enjoy anything I do? How will I be able to carry on in my job?" This is a good point. If you were bored, uninterested, and indifferent every day at work, it would make good sense not to come in to work. But here is the mess that blues victims create for themselves. They argue that if they cannot be inspired and stimulated on the job today, then they will never be. This is utter nonsense. Although you may not be motivated today, you can still perform. You are still capable of doing your job—and doing it reasonably well. Tomorrow you may feel the exact opposite of what you feel today. But for the blues victim, it has to happen, with guarantees that inspiration will occur regularly. There will be many occasions when we are not inspired to complete certain tasks. But we can still do them with a fair degree of success and gain satisfaction from the fact that we were able to complete them under conditions that were not ideal.

10. Risks

A final point to consider is that it is advisable to take risks in other areas of your life. Blues victims tend to specialize in one area and one area alone: work. They do this for two significant reasons. First, they consider themselves to be experts in their respective jobs. As experts, they cannot help but succeed, or so they believe. The expectation of success, therefore, motivates them to continue to specialize in work. They are most comfortable on the job. They think they know what is going to happen there. They presume success is going to be their prize. They take for granted that they are going to get all the accompanying rewards. The second and more important reason these victims specialize in work is their fear of failing in other areas of life. That is why they don't socialize, dance, take up hobbies, try sports, or do anything else. They fear that their performance may be only average. If they cannot be outstanding at what they do and get the rewards that come with an outstanding performance, then what is the point of trying? So they don't try to have fun for the sake of having fun. If they cannot be guaranteed success, forget it.

Thus, blues victims reduce their worlds to what goes on in the workplace. This is their first home, their hiding place. This is where they feel wanted and needed, where they will ultimately realize all their dreams. But what happens if their dreams are not fulfilled? They burn out and at times get seriously depressed.

Isn't it curious that many people immediately suffer health problems, including heart attacks, after they retire? Who is to say exactly what contributes to their health problems? But I think it would be safe to surmise that, because these people placed so much importance on their work and took little risk elsewhere, it caught up to them. Once retired, they became desperate, fearful, worried, anxious, and distressed, and these emotions probably have a considerable effect on their health.

So, blues victims beware! Take risks in life. There are many payoffs. You will more than likely do a better job when you are working, and you may be healthier when you are no longer working. Once you involve yourself in activities outside of work, you will place fewer demands on your job. You will not expect it to give you everything that you want out of life. You will be able to approach the workplace in a more-reasonable fashion and enjoy what the rest of life has to offer. It will make the workplace a more satisfying environment.

A banker whom I counseled eventually came to a conclusion that helped him overcome his problem almost overnight:

> I always expected too much, but worse than that, I demanded that these expectations be met. Perfection was a critical demand. I made it very clear to my staff at work and to my family at home that things better be done right and done right the first time. Job success was another necessary demand that had to be fulfilled. I placed my work ahead of everything, including my family. I knew that this was the only way to get recognition and advancement. To this day, I'm not sure why my family put up with it. But the only thing that mattered to me was work and more work. All I would ever dream about was greater productivity and greater success. If my demands were not met, for whatever reason, I became a holy tyrant. People were blasted if they did not live up to my expectations. After all, I did not push people any harder than I pushed myself. In fact, I drove myself crazy trying to meet all of the many self-imposed urgencies. If I didn't do everything just so, I would tear the hide off my back with verbal self-abuse.

One day, my whole world crashed around me. This happened when I was overlooked for what I believed was a major promotion. How could the company do this to me after all I had done for it? I went into such a depression that I could barely pull myself in to work. I truly was broken down.

Then it struck me: The company didn't owe me anything. Anyway, they had been very good to me over the years. It was just me. My family had been telling me this for years, but I never had the time or patience to listen. It was these crazy ideas that had possessed me for so long that led to my depression. But now I no longer had to hang on to these demands, nor did I have to act this way. Oh, work would always be important to me and I would put forth my best effort, but now I would set limits, which I had never done before. It was time to discard these crazy work habits and at the same time enjoy my family and the rest of the world out there. And you know what? I was sure that I would be better on the job!

Considering everything that has been discussed, what should you aim for? You should aim for a philosophical shift. If this sounds imposing, it isn't meant to be. It simply means that you should take a look at your exaggerated expectations and extreme beliefs and go out of your way to alter them. Debunk. Reduce their exaggerated, cynical, and pessimistic qualities. Generate more-moderate ideas. Once this is done, living in the workplace and at home becomes considerably easier. And, surprisingly enough, although blues victims may still doubt this, performance will be as good as, if not better than, it previously was. This also means, and blues victims may still be shocked by this, that you will be more likely to succeed. Shape what goes on in your head. Change the extreme so that it becomes more moderate. A big pay off is waiting for you: You are going to feel a lot better, and you are going to perform more capably. And, most important, your blues will gradually fade away.

At this point you can shed the label "blues victim." Once you dedicate yourself to taking charge of your career and to managing your environment at work and outside more effectively, you are no longer a "victim."

8 Things Do Not Happen; Things Are Made to Happen

John F. Kennedy

Building a Social Support System

Communication and dialogue imply sharing your thoughts and feelings with those who are important to you. People who are depressed invariably isolate themselves. They are ashamed and embarrassed; they feel foolish. They believe that they have let themselves down, along with their communities, their families, their colleagues, and their companies. As a result, they bottle up their feelings inside and hope that with the passage of time everything will get better. That rarely happens.

There is tremendous merit in opening up. Someone who is recovering from the blues may find this very awkward. However, the more you experiment, the easier it becomes. You don't have to share your thoughts and feelings with the whole world. You don't have to run up to every colleague in the workplace and say: "I want to talk to you about my feelings and my innermost thoughts." Open up to those you trust and feel close to.

Talking about feeling down is important, both for the open expression of feelings and thoughts and for the admission to yourself and key people around you that you have a problem. You are facing up to your embarrassment and shame. You are finally realizing that there is no value in denying your problem. You can now begin to share what you have experienced—the expectations that have been fulfilled and those that have not, the things that have worked out for you and those that have not. You can finally reveal your disappointments, disillusionments, losses, and defeats. In essence, you must form a social support system. We have always assumed that family and relatives are very important in our social support system. However, it is becoming more commonplace to include work colleagues and managers in the social support network. This does not mean that you are going to be indiscriminate about whom you choose to include in your network. You want to include certain key people in whom you have faith. We are beginning to fully understand that people who have strong social support systems seem over the long term to suffer less from pressure and the blues. In a sense, support networks act as barriers to the blues and depression.

We have always known that so-called "underground communication systems" exist in the workplace. These systems occur only in private surroundings, with considerable secrecy. They involve gatherings of workers and colleagues who quietly carry on closed-door conversations about what is going on in any given department, unit, or organization. In a sense, these units act as social support networks. What may occur in the future is that these underground networks will surface and social support systems will become an accepted part of organizations.

It may be happening already. "Quality circles" could be described as very fundamental social support groups. Although they address issues related to problem solving and task completion, they nonetheless deal in basic terms with the frustrations and worries that people experience, which impede the progress of quality work. Obviously you cannot sit around in your place of work and talk about problems, fears, and worries indefinitely. That would not be very productive. Guidelines would be needed to outline how much time would be devoted to a discussion of feelings and how much to an analysis of potential solutions to emotional problems. Otherwise, you would have a "sensitivity group" on your hands, where people would simply vent their feelings and nothing more. Who needs that mess?

As companies become more enlightened, these support groups will become more legitimate entities. With the sharing of feelings and thoughts and the offer of feedback, employees will realize that their painful feelings and exaggerated thoughts are not uncommon. The encouragement and support that certain colleagues and managers can give can go a long way to helping an unhappy person become a productive member of the team once again.

Choices, Choices, and More Choices

People who are suffering from the blues believe that they have
only one option: to push, drive, and overtax their bodies and
minds. Then they can trample adversity and make a comeback.
But we know that the only thing that gets trampled is the person.
Other choices do exist. Some alternatives are helpful; others are
destructive. Certain choices can exacerbate the blues; others go
a long way toward bringing about healthy and positive changes.
These choices are detailed in the following sections.

DIVERSION

The first option is diversion. A diversion is an activity that is
designed to divert your attention away from a particular difficulty. It involves virtually no shift whatsoever in your beliefs or
expectations. Examples of diversions include a weekend break,
athletics, jogging, partying, a trip—any activity that does not
directly address your particular concerns.

What are the dangers of diversions? You may get so wrapped
up in your particular diversion that you deny that you have a problem. A diversion offers temporary relief from your difficulties. This
temporary relief becomes extremely satisfying and gratifying. It feels
great to get away from the hassles of work. It feels so good that you
are tempted to do it over and over and over again. The diversion
itself begins to supply you with delusions of grandeur. This activity
may become so utterly consuming that you look forward to nothing
else. It takes on addictive properties, like certain drugs.

All of this might sound far-fetched but, in fact, a number of people who are suffering from the blues have become psychologically addicted to their particular diversion. It gives them a tremendous emotional high, which they want to experience continuously.

I once counseled a building contractor who had suffered a heart attack. Fortunately, he made a quick and complete recovery. I saw him afterward, and we discussed the events that led up to the heart attack. We discovered that he was depressed both at work and at home. His life did not seem to have much meaning. He was also overweight. He was fed up with his career, his home life, and himself. He decided to take up jogging. He jogged regularly each and every day. He became so involved with jogging that it almost became a compulsion. At the same time, he made no effort to confront his problem, preferring to avoid it altogether. As he was jogging, he also began to notice that he was losing more and more weight. This reinforced his belief that he should continue to run regularly. He ran with intensity, vigor, determination and, finally, compulsively. Just prior to the heart attack, he began to notice discomfort and pain while he was jogging. His body was telling him to slow down, but he did not pay attention to the signals. He kept on running, obsessed with and controlled by his accomplishments. One day, while jogging, he collapsed.

I am not suggesting that his heart attack was caused by his jogging. Many factors probably contributed to it, including a family history of heart problems. He did, however, approach jogging in a very compulsive fashion, to the detriment of everything else in his life. He also chose to disregard the messages that his body was sending him. He opted for the addictive pleasures of jogging, until one day he suffered the consequences.

Variations on this particular story are repeated every day. Individuals choose diversions not because they truly enjoy them, but because through them they can escape from their problems. The results can be tragic. People with the blues sometimes choose very dangerous diversions, such as skydiving, mountain climbing, and race car driving. You might think that these people just crave some excitement in their lives. That may be true, but why do these people suddenly choose risky activities when they are trying to wrestle with their problems.

There are a host of other, less dangerous activities that people who are coping with the blues can choose. Some examples include golfing, cycling, swimming, tennis, and weightlifting. These activities are very healthy. They all involve physical exertion to a greater or lesser degree, which does seem to promote good health. But when they become too absorbing and engulfing, they can become hazardous to your health.

PARTYING

Partying constitutes another popular diversion. Some people are always in search of a party. It is almost as if they work in order to party. They are burned out on the job and burned out at home, so there is really nothing left except partying. Where there are parties, there is often booze, and at times drugs. Instead of coming to grips with their problems, some people resort to these extreme diversions. But their difficulties usually get worse.

Be careful. Ask yourself why you are engaged in your particular diversion. If it is because you enjoy it, and not because you are running away from something else, then there is little danger. But if you choose this activity because it is an easy way out, because it allows you to temporarily forget about your problems, you are endangering yourself. This activity may become so consuming that you never work out your blues problem and, as a result, suffer some serious health problems in the process.

INTROSPECTION

The next option might be described as major introspection. In short, you spend considerable time thinking. You may be examining those beliefs and expectations that are extreme in an attempt to reshape them so that they become more reasonable. But there is a trap here. Certain people who are coping with the blues get too caught up in the deliberation process. They become navel-gazers, spending far too much time and energy pondering, brooding, reflecting, and mulling over their problems. In a sense, they are caught up in cerebral jogging. They become so addicted to thinking that they do nothing else. This behavior is almost as dangerous a trap as the previous choice. Although introspection may not be as damaging to your physical health, it does not help bring about any positive changes in your life. Introspection simply affords you the opportunity to find out what you are "all about." It gives you a chance to assess what is going on in your head. Beyond that, introspection does not guarantee action and thus has definite limitations.

BALANCE

Striving for balance is a sensible choice. People coping with the blues go out of their way to spend a portion of their time changing their beliefs and expectations so that these beliefs and expectations become more reasonable. After that, they spend additional time figuring out how to do things differently. The balance option apportions time so that some is devoted to mind and some to behavior.

How does one go about changing behavior? The same behavioral techniques for combating pressure that we discussed in Chapter 3 can be quite useful for blues sufferers, as well. They include self-declaration, win-win negotiation, dialoguing, problem-solving, risk-taking, and time management. Mounds of books and articles have been written about these particular techniques, and many courses offer training in these areas. Once you change your philosophical approach, you will be in a better position to bring about some changes in your workplace. You also will be in a better position to create changes in your working relationships with colleagues and management. Going out of your way to improve yourself and your working environment is beneficial for you and for those with whom you work. So you win, and your organization wins.

BAIL-OUT

Occasionally, people coping with the blues unfortunately resort to bailing out of the situation. Bail-out is very tempting because it has specific short-term benefits. When you bail out, you no longer have to deal with the problem. People may choose to transfer from a particular department or quit the organization. They may change jobs on a regular basis. It is not unusual to find them hopping from their first career to a second, then to a third, and so on. Some people never seem to be able to settle down. They always seem driven in the pursuit of ultimate triumph. If they cannot get it in one environment, they are determined to get it somewhere else. The commitment factor is not there; they are simply committed to bailing out. Some people dealing with the blues do the same thing in their private lives. They are constantly changing relationships, friendships, and residences. Their whole life is one big bail-out.

However, very little thought goes into the reasons behind this behavior. If you do not sit down and spend some time figuring out why you are bailing out and what direction your life is taking, you will accomplish very little. There will be no value and no long-term benefits to your behavior. People who jump around thoughtlessly end up in a similar mess most of the time. Although they hop from job to job, the same problems recur. They skip from relationship to relationship, but the same hassles emerge. Throughout these escapades, they still have not fully recovered from the symptoms and pain of the blues. So bail-out is a dangerous ploy.

REGROUPING

The final option may be described as a total regrouping. This major choice is a very useful one. It is not necessarily worthwhile for all people, but it certainly is for those who have attempted to change their working environment and have found the results unsatisfactory. The ultimate answer is to leave, which may involve permanently transferring out of your department or quitting your company and looking for work elsewhere.

This option is different from bail-out in that people have spent some time thinking and have changed certain beliefs and expectations that are too extreme. They have made changes in how they behave and have tried to alter certain aspects of their jobs with which they are unhappy. These may include job description, reporting relationships, workload, task responsibility, and so on. If the results are unsatisfactory, then total regrouping is a workable and viable option.

Certain people have been very satisfied with this choice. They recognize that they no longer fit the organization. These people ended up leaving on very reasonable terms. They were satisfied, the organization was satisfied, and they kept in touch. Thus, total regrouping can be a very productive choice, both for the individual and for the company.

You have now had an opportunity to consider a number of choices. It would appear that the options of balance and total regrouping have the greatest likelihood of producing both long-term and short-term gains. The other choices—diversion, major introspection, and bail-out—are flawed because they keep you from facing up to your problems. Look for the option that will produce the best results for you and experiment with it!

The Three Hs

HAPPINESS

Some programs are currently being offered on the topic of happiness training. Can you believe it—training people to be happy? Does that tell you something about our society? About our workforce?

Let's examine the fundamental principles of this happiness-training course. The key tenets include:

- Stop worrying.
- Be yourself.
- Develop positive and optimistic thinking.
- Remain busy and keep active.
- Spend more time socializing with others.
- Lower your expectations, aspirations, and demands.
- Become present oriented, not future or past oriented.

When you examine these principles, they make a lot of sense. Does the presence of happiness training courses mean that too many people today are unhappy and therefore require happiness training? Does it mean that we are all a miserable lot and therefore require regeneration? Does it mean that we don't even know what happiness is about and therefore require some new skills training? Or does it simply mean that we need some upgrading in the way we create our own happiness? Whatever the reason for the creation of happiness training, the fundamental concepts are reasonable and well advised. These basic guidelines reinforce many of the ideas that have been discussed in this book. So don't be too surprised if you see an advertisement in your local paper offering a course on happiness training.

HARDINESS

Now that you have gained control over your blues, what should you strive for? There is a new buzzword: hardiness. If we can have hardy plants, we can certainly have hardy people. But what is actually meant by hardiness?

The first principle of hardiness is to commit yourself to thinking, feeling, and doing, but not necessarily to succeeding. There is a tremendous difference. Blues victims are totally and completely committed to succeeding. The new, hardy person will be more dedicated to thinking, feeling, and doing, and therefore will likely succeed more often. It makes sense. If you are devoted to understanding yourself better and doing the best job you can, you will probably be more successful in all areas of your life, especially your work.

The second principle of hardiness is to commit yourself to overall happiness, not specifically to glory and grandeur. Blues victims religiously commit themselves to going after the honor and splendor that can be acquired only through success in the workplace. The new hardy employee will go after the whole ball of wax. He will be dedicated to achieving overall happiness, which will include activities both within and outside the workplace. The advantage of this approach is that happiness spreads. If you are happy outside the workplace, you bring that joy with you into the workplace. If you are high-spirited inside the workplace, you take that happiness outside.

The third guiding principle of hardiness is to pursue challenges in all aspects of your life, not just in one. Blues victims run after achievement in the workplace. The hardy person will be challenged by a wide variety of opportunities both on and off the job. She will find it easier to handle the ups and downs that occur on the job because of her many outside interests. She will be able to ride the crest of fulfillment when the work is rewarding and weather the troughs of nonfulfillment when the work is routine.

A fourth principle of hardiness is to develop a strong support system. Blues victims are social isolates. They cannot tolerate the embarrassment and shame of failure, so they separate themselves from others. Furthermore, they blame the world, the workplace, their colleagues, their managers, and their families for their woes. This means that they remain detached from everyone because they were so angry with so many people.

The hardy person will cultivate a strong social network. This support network will include trusted key colleagues with whom to share feelings and thoughts and come away with a better perspective on matters in the workplace. After all, whether we are prepared to admit it, we are all social animals, and relationships are important, especially in the workplace. Once this strong support system is established, the hardy person will find it easier to maintain a consistently high level of productivity.

HUMOR

Humor and laughter are very important. Humor has the capacity to change your perspective. It involves a new outlook, a transformation in the way that you view things. When you laugh, when you see the lighter side of a situation, you have altered your attitude and your perception. Because you have changed your mind-set and have placed limitations on your seriousness, you can finally declare that situations and events no longer control you. In essence, you can control a situation by choosing how somberly you react. Blues victims are inordinately somber in every aspect of their lives, particularly their working lives. By limiting your seriousness, you introduce a more flexible frame of mind that will enhance performance. Because you are not locked in by your seriousness, you are able to roll with the punches. In a sense, you are master of your environment.

Some of you might think that only mediocre people have a good sense of humor. They can afford to laugh because they have nothing at stake. Those who are interested in success, however, cannot afford to be humorous. This is utter nonsense. Did you know, for example, that people with a sense of humor are usually more innovative, more willing to embrace new ideas and opportunities, and usually perform far better? They generally achieve their goals and get along well with people. Did you also know that upper-level managers are usually regarded as having the best sense of humor?

If that doesn't turn you on, maybe this will. Researchers have suggested that humor and laughter can reduce your susceptibility to physical illness and disease. If you have a good sense of humor and laugh regularly, you may be releasing healing hormones that can help you to maintain your health.

Norman Cousins, former editor of *Saturday Review* magazine, had a very serious illness. His health was gradually deteriorating, and the attending doctors believed that he would not recover. As he contemplated what to do about his condition, Mr. Cousins decided that if negative emotions can contribute to one's vulnerability to illness, then positive emotions can contribute to one's likelihood of recovery. He started to watch all types of funny films. As he continued to laugh on a regular basis, he noticed that his health improved dramatically. I am not suggesting that his laughter was the only factor that caused his health to improve. But he himself felt that humor and laughter played a large part in his recovery.

Is this, then, not reason enough to consider humor and laughter? There are now conferences devoted solely to the power of laughter, play, and humor. If you have forgotten how to laugh, you might want to go to one of these conferences. In any case, be sure to incorporate humor into your everyday activities. Look in the mirror. If you don't have laugh lines on your face, make certain that you start laughing more regularly.

The Approach to Solving the Problem Can't Be the Same Approach That Created the Problem

If you believe you are suffering from the blues, consider doing the following: Step back from your situation. Cool off. Take an objective look at things.

After you have stepped back, decide quickly how blue you are by asking yourself the series of questions that were listed at the beginning of the section on the blues. If you answer "yes" to most of these questions, you have some problems to tackle.

The next step is to examine your beliefs and expectations. Determine which beliefs are extreme and exaggerated and thus threatening your well-being. Once you have decided which expectations are the culprits, then proceed to reduce their demanding and intense qualities. This will make you feel considerably better.

After you have changed your outlook and perspective, talk to someone you trust. It may simply mean going next door to a close colleague's office, shutting the door behind you, and sharing a feeling or thought. While you are talking with your colleague, you might consider the options that are available to you. In fact, you could discuss your choices with your colleague.

Once you have followed these steps, you may find that the blues have changed color. So take control of your life. Take charge of what happens to you in the workplace and outside. Rejoice in becoming an excellent blues master.

> Don't Let the Fear of Striking
> Out Hold You Back
>
> **Babe Ruth**

To summarize:

1. COOL OFF

Remove yourself from whatever you're doing and calm down.

2. ASSESS

Determine how upset you are by taking an inventory of your feelings and thoughts.

3. DEBUNK

Identify and then dispute your unhealthy ideas and replace them with healthier, more realistic thoughts.

4. DIALOGUE

Make a point of opening up to someone you trust.

5. SELECT

Make a choice that is helpful and productive, with short-term and long-term benefits.

6. SUPPORT

Build a network of people who you believe are trustworthy and with whom you can exchange thoughts, expectations, and feelings.

Once again, hold yourself accountable by rewarding yourself for new choices taken, for example, going on a short trip you've always wanted to take, buying yourself a home entertainment unit, or punishing yourself for failing to face the problem by donating to a charity that you dislike or visiting a friend or family member you have avoided for a long time.

> There Is a Great Deal of Unmapped
> Country Within Us
>
> **George Eliot**

Life offers you choices. You have a choice with respect to how you negotiate your workplace. You can be pressured, blue, and depressed, or you can be reasonably happy and productive and enjoy a meaningful career. The choice is basically in your hands.

Have you ever asked yourself why certain people are happier, healthier, and more productive? If you are like most individuals, you probably have. Maybe you came up with some interesting answers. We are discovering that people who are healthier, happier, and more productive have different beliefs and expectations. Their minds are filled with a considerable amount of flexibility, tolerance, patience, and rationality and a tremendous sense of humor. I believe that all of us know people like that. Sometimes we marvel at them. We wonder how they can work in the midst of chaos, turmoil, disruption, and change and yet come out of the experience with smiles on their faces. These people seem to display a sense of assurance and peace that is almost spiritual in nature.

What goes on in your head largely determines how you feel, what you do, how successful you are, and whether you are at peace with yourself. What is equally exciting, if not more so, is that you can choose to think what you wish to think, expect what you wish to expect, and believe what you wish to believe. Moreover, you can change your thinking, your expectations, and your beliefs. You can debunk! If you are unhappy and unproductive at work or outside, you can go inside your head and figure out what is going on. Once you make the necessary changes, you can determine how to manage your life differently. The results will probably be most rewarding, gratifying, and exciting. The events in your life will no longer control you; you will control them.

When you can master pressure and the blues effectively, you can truly derive pleasure from your experiences. You can begin to appreciate the challenges you face. You can enjoy the opportunities, the friendships, and the unpredictable nature of change. After all, isn't this what life, let alone work, is all about?

Blues-Proofing Roadmap

Here is your roadmap to blues-proofing so that you resolve your issues and increase your health and well-being.

Record the concern you want to work on. Be specific. The questionnaires in the Appendix section may be helpful. Complete as many as you need to help you decide the key matter that requires your attention.

_____

Record the debunking you use to counteract your unhealthy thinking about the concern that triggered your blues or depression.

_____

_____

Record the healthy thoughts and self-talk you use to overcome your problem.

_____

_____

Imagine you have just solved your problem. Record where you are and what you are doing. Be precise. This becomes the solution you now go after.

_____

_____

Record the new action that you will pursue to achieve the solution.

Action _____ by date ..../..../....

Action _____ by date ..../..../....

Identify people who are trustworthy and how they will help you.

Person _____Helpful action _____

Person _____Helpful action _____

THREE

Postscript

From the Organization's Viewpoint

9 Shaping the Pressure- and Blues-Free Company

Getting the Edge in a Global Economy

I would be remiss if I did not comment on the organizations of the future. Those companies that are able to create environments in which pressure and the blues are minimized will likely be more successful, more productive, and more effective at achieving their goals than those that ignore these problems.

Today we have been exposed to many management principles and theories. We're told that we should value and recognize our workers. We hear that people are our main resource. We know from the many books, magazine articles, and studies on management styles, strategies, and the corporate culture that it is critical to develop a workforce team that is committed to productivity and to the success of the organization. At the same time, we realize that change is all around us—that we must learn to manage change. We have moved from the industrial era to the information era. We are overwhelmed by information and bombarded by technological advancement that further contributes to information overload.

We are also aware that nations and corporations are moving from a nation-based economy to a global economy. We can no longer restrict our planning, production, and marketing strategies to our own borders, or even to the borders of neighboring countries. We must now develop a strategy that recognizes the globe as our region of trade. Furthermore, we are competing with nations that seem able to produce various products more efficiently and more economically than we can. Competition in the marketplace has never been stiffer.

As a consequence of all these shifts in our corporate society, it is critical that the workforce be as happy, healthy, and productive as possible to face the challenges ahead.

Many business leaders and managers still believe that people should leave their problems at home. If you, as an employee, are pressured, blue, or depressed, don't bring your garbage to work! Just put your nose to the grindstone and keep on producing! This kind of reasoning belongs to an earlier age and should be left to the history books.

Today, people are interested in careers, not jobs. They are interested in the meaningful nature of their work. They are also interested in a variety of other factors to which management does not pay sufficient attention People want to know that their organizations care about them and are concerned about their welfare.

People want to know that their organizations are trying to make the work environment stimulating and satisfying. If people sense that their companies are putting out, people themselves will put out. If workers believe their companies are committed to them, they commit themselves to their companies. If organizations are committed to the health and well-being of their people, the people will be committed to the health and well-being of the organizations. Once this happens, you can rest assured that the organization will indeed be healthy, productive, and on the leading edge of its field.

In the future, those companies at the forefront, organizations with healthy workforces that are prepared to compete, corporations that meet most of their goals and objectives, will have the following controls in place:

First, companies will make available to their people the opportunity to have emotional checkups, just as we now have physical checkups. People will consult with professionals who systematically assess their behavior, the pressures they are experiencing, and their blues potential. If an examination reveals that the person is suffering too much pressure or is depressed, then he or she will get appropriate help.

Second, companies will have emotional-control centers, although they might not be called by that name. They might be called counseling centers, holistic health centers, or employee assistance programs (EAPs). Professionals at these centers will provide help to people who are experiencing tension, anxiety, blues, depression, or other related problems. Over the past three decades, EAPs have been the fastest growing workplace health service. Today it is fair to state that approximately 75% of North American companies have some form of EAP available to their people.

In addition to these services, health education and health promotion programs will be available in the workplace. People will be taught by professionals how to prevent unreasonable patterns of thought from invading their minds. Furthermore, they will be taught to maintain a course of positive health and "wellness." Once again, many North American companies currently have some form of wellness programming available to their workers, whether it be in the form of lectures, workshops, lunch-and-learn sessions or more comprehensive behavioral change programs.

Third, organizations will endorse the establishment and maintenance of support networks in the workplace. These groups—call them "circles" if you wish—will be devoted to sharing expectations, thoughts, beliefs, values, and problem-solving ideas regarding work-related issues. They will be structured around basic goals and objectives. These groups will meet as the need arises. The agenda typically will be geared to helping individuals work through problems that are inhibiting personal productivity.

Fourth, companies will value peoples' participation in the various health-related programs and support groups. This will be reflected in their performance appraisals. Companies will make very clear that overall ratings will take into account not only performance but also employees' willingness to care for their health and well-being.

Fifth, corporations will value thinking as much as, if not more than, doing. Organizations will not only ask people how much they got done but also how much time they spent thinking about and planning their projects. People will be rewarded not just for working harder but also for working smarter.

Sixth, companies will value laughter and a good sense of humor. Presentations will receive better reviews if they incorporate appropriate humor. Through the appraisal process, people will receive points for maintaining a balanced perspective that incorporates flexibility, tolerance, patience, and keen wit.

Reading this, you might say to yourself, "Come on, now! These are only the wild ramblings of a crazy psychologist! None of this is really feasible, let alone practical or workable. And who really needs to do this?" Well, companies that value their workforces will do this. And if you think that these practices are not feasible, you might be surprised to know that they are already in operation! EAPs and wellness programs are very common among North American organizations, and maybe the rest is just around the corner. So think and act quickly, because many enlightened organizations are already beating you to the punch!

Pressure- and Blues-Proofing Through Web-Based Training

Throughout the book, we have discussed effective ways in which individuals can remove pressures and the blues to improve their working and personal lives. However, organizational leaders also have expressed concern about the steps they need to take to address employee pressures, anxieties, and related difficulties. There are legitimate reasons for their concerns. Current workplace research (*Corporate Ethics Monitor*, 2005; Watson Wyatt Survey, 2005; Economic Business Roundtable, 2006) consistently confirms that 15% to 20% of the workforce experiences behavioral problems, including anxiety, stress, and depression. These maladies cost organizations a great deal of money and productivity. People with problems have two to four times higher absentee rates, have six times higher accident rates, and collect three times higher sickness and accident benefits. Employers lose many billions of dollars in direct disability and workers' compensation costs and bear the burden of indirect costs related to worker replacement, decreased productivity, and overtime.

In addition, people with pressure and anxiety problems

- are late for work more often
- have serious interpersonal problems more frequently
- perform at only 50% to 75% of their potential
- negatively impact the morale and the working lives of those around them
- generate more lawsuits and arbitration hearings

These problems cost public and private sector organizations many billions of dollars annually, a figure that is of grave concern to business leaders who are striving for efficiencies and savings so that they can remain competitive in the marketplace.

In response, organizational leaders have over the years established support and resource services in the form of EAPs, enhanced occupational health programs, and improved human resources functions, with the assumption that employees in trouble would access these services if needed. And indeed people have accessed these programs in droves, with positive results overall.

Business leaders also reasoned that if preventive steps were implemented, then the duration and seriousness of employee problems could be minimized or short-circuited altogether. Thus, training and development programs for managers and supervisors have been implemented over the past two decades to teach them the skills necessary to address employee problems. Managers and supervisors are in the best position to monitor daily activities of employees and observe any changes in functioning. They are the first line of defense for their staff and have the most salient and immediate impact on the people who report to them.

However, traditional training has been costly, time consuming, and a burden, because participants are often required to spend time away from their workplaces. Traditional training designed to improve participants' performance on the job often involves 1 to 3 days of work outside the office in a group setting, with a trainer at the front of a room who takes the participants through a series of lectures and paper-and-pencil exercises with a lot of handouts. Training fees can vary from $1,000 to $2,000 per trainee for courses on "How to Deal with Troubled Employees."

Additionally, the results of traditional training have been disappointing because there has been little skill transfer to the workplace and, despite the training, managers and supervisors have continued to handle employee issues in the same, ineffective fashion—namely, they overlook, avoid, ignore, deny, or use the "geographical cure" by transferring the person out of the work group.

Realizing the shortcomings of traditional training, The Berkeley Centre for Effectiveness (TBCE), a consulting organization that specializes in creating and implementing unique, Web-based training programs, devoted its resources to developing a self-paced, self-directed learning solution that would allow trainees in small-, medium-, and large-sized organizations to learn at their desks and even in the comfort of their homes after work. The extremely efficient, cost-effective solution that evolved is Behaviour Risk Management (BRM), a Web-based training module that allows managers and supervisors to deal with employee problems.

After more than 2 years of research, development, and field-testing, the BRM training module is ready for the marketplace. It is a step-by-step program that managers and supervisors can use with at-risk employees who are experiencing pressure, the blues, depression, and related problems. It offers a user-friendly guide consisting of two components: the course itself and the direct application of tools and techniques described in the course. BRM trains users how to identify relevant behavior risks, interview effectively, intervene appropriately, document the process, and follow-up on and evaluate employee behavior changes. It is highly engaging and interactive and can be used as often as needed, for as many times as needed, until it becomes part of the supervisor's repertoire. This helps ensure that employee skills are utilized effectively.

Rather than $1,000 to $2,000 per trainee, the cost is $5 to $50 per trainee, depending on the size of the employee base.

BRM provides the tools and skill set needed to

- reduce workplace conflicts
- promote awareness of behavioral issues
- enhance health and safety knowledge
- reduce absenteeism
- reduce accident and disability claims
- reduce training costs
- decrease the financial drain on companies
- improve supervisory and management skills
- increase productivity
- provide a reference guide to managers with respect to structured interventions
- improve communication and dialogue

Ultimately, the BRM program aims to strengthen the relationship between employee and supervisor. The supervisor, maybe for the first time, will have the confidence to constructively help the employee in trouble. In turn, the employee will hopefully trust the process enough to include the supervisor as a part of the support network helping him to overcome pressure, the blues, and other issues. This Web-based BRM training program should greatly assist the pressure- and blues-proofing process, and we at TBCE are very excited about this new offering to the marketplace.

Appendix

In the pressure-proofing and blues-proofing roadmaps, reference was made to questionnaires at the back of the book. On the next 10 pages, you will find scales designed to help you decide what area requires your attention for change. You may want to complete all of them or just one or two. Each scale has a number of questions with three possible choices opposite each item. Circle the response that best represents what you believe to be true. There are no "right" or "wrong" answers.

After completing the questions, total your score by adding the numbers that you have circled and record it in the space opposite "My total score." Then move on to the next scale, completing as many scales as you wish.

The scales with the lowest totals indicate areas that require change. A score below 30 on any scale requires immediate attention; otherwise, pressure, the blues, anxiety, and depression will follow you everywhere.

Work

	No	Sometimes	Yes
I enjoy going into work each day.	1	2	3
My supervisor and I are able to communicate.	1	2	3
I am enthusiastic about my work.	1	2	3
I work well with my peers.	1	2	3
If I am in a jam, I can count on my colleagues.	1	2	3
I constantly want to be somewhere other than at work.	3	2	1
I have a lot of work to do, but I can handle it.	1	2	3
Management is honest and treats me fairly.	1	2	3
Work seems meaningless to me right now.	3	2	1
I am usually rewarded for work well done.	1	2	3
My colleagues are no longer as enjoyable to be with.	3	2	1
As a team, we work well and support one another.	1	2	3
Many changes are happening at work, but I am able to cope with them.	1	2	3
Work has lost its appeal.	3	2	1
I am managing my pressure well.	1	2	3
My total score			_____

Career

	No	Sometimes	Yes
I regularly review my career aspirations.	1	2	3
I have lost interest in my career.	3	2	1
I update my résumé to ensure that it reflects recent career changes.	1	2	3
I rely on management to look after my career.	3	2	1
I make a point of meeting regularly with management to discuss career development opportunities.	1	2	3
I know where my career is going.	1	2	3
I don't have time to pay close attention to my career.	3	2	1
I take responsibility for my career and do not rely on my employer to do so.	1	2	3
I maintain a good network of peers and colleagues to keep abreast of trends and opportunities.	1	2	3
I don't enjoy speaking to others about my career.	3	2	1
I talk with my partner about my career goals and future plans.	1	2	3
I can count on my support network when I am uncertain about my next career move.	1	2	3
There is a healthy balance between my career and my home life.	1	2	3
There is no direction to where my career is going.	3	2	1
I am fulfilling my career ambitions.	1	2	3
My total score			_____

Management

	No	Sometimes	Yes
I am able to talk with my manager.	1	2	3
I avoid my manager.	3	2	1
My manager rewards me for work that I do well.	1	2	3
I find that I am too closely managed.	3	2	1
My manager is well organized and expects the same from me.	1	2	3
My manager takes advantage of me.	3	2	1
My manager does not take the time to listen to me.	3	2	1
My manager is interested in working with me to advance my career.	1	2	3
I am able to honestly voice my concerns to my manager.	1	2	3
My manager finds it easier to criticize than to recognize.	3	2	1
I feel awkward around my manager.	3	2	1
I have little input in decision making.	3	2	1
I don't know where I stand with my manager.	3	2	1
My manager is fair with me.	1	2	3
My manager supports my efforts to get ahead.	1	2	3
My total score			_____

Recognition

	No	Sometimes	Yes
I am recognized for work well done.	1	2	3
Management's style is to criticize.	3	2	1
I rarely receive feedback about the work I've done.	3	2	1
My colleagues acknowledge my efforts.	1	2	3
My peers are very competitive and highly critical of one another.	3	2	1
I don't trust my supervisor to cooperate with me.	3	2	1
I feel valued by my peers.	1	2	3
The work I do is important to the organization.	1	2	3
My job does not offer opportunity for advancement.	3	2	1
I am respected for the work I do.	1	2	3
I reward myself when I finish what I do.	1	2	3
Others recognize the pressures I'm experiencing and the extra work that I'm carrying.	1	2	3
Management doesn't acknowledge all that I have accomplished.	3	2	1
I feel dumped on a lot.	3	2	1
My colleagues acknowledge each other's strengths and as such we work well as a team.	1	2	3
My total score			_____

Communication

	No	Sometimes	Yes
Communication is nonexistent in my organization.	3	2	1
Our group holds regular meetings to discuss workplace issues.	1	2	3
Management keeps us informed of key issues.	1	2	3
People are too secretive.	3	2	1
I find that I keep things to myself.	3	2	1
People don't trust one another.	3	2	1
I am free to voice my concerns to management.	1	2	3
There is no openness in our group.	3	2	1
Management often keeps me out of the loop.	3	2	1
I am comfortable asking for help from others.	1	2	3
I am comfortable seeking advice from my manager.	1	2	3
I have no one to discuss difficult situations with.	3	2	1
I have no trouble expressing my uncomfortable feelings with others.	1	2	3
I let others know when I am upset.	1	2	3
I avoid others rather than openly talking to them about what bugs me.	1	2	3
My total score			_____

Intimacy

	No	Sometimes	Yes
I am pleased with my relationship.	1	2	3
My partner and I are open and honest with one another.	1	2	3
I often get angry with my partner.	3	2	1
My partner and I are sexually compatible.	1	2	3
I feel listened to in my relationship.	1	2	3
My partner and I share very little.	3	2	1
My partner and I solve problems together well.	1	2	3
My partner and I are compassionate and understanding.	1	2	3
I am drifting away from my partner.	3	2	1
There is depth to our relationship.	1	2	3
I find my partner easy to talk to.	1	2	3
I have no patience for my partner.	3	2	1
We enjoy each other's company.	1	2	3
My mind wanders when my partner speaks to me.	3	2	1
I am confident about the future of our relationship.	1	2	3
My total score			_____

Family

	No	Sometimes	Yes
I have a meaningful relationship with my children.	1	2	3
My parents and I do not have a good relationship.	3	2	1
My in-laws and I enjoy each other's company.	1	2	3
I am drifting away from my family.	3	2	1
As a family, we resolve our disputes well.	1	2	3
My spouse and I don't get along with our teenage children.	3	2	1
My parents and in-laws get along well together.	1	2	3
I am uneasy and uptight at home.	3	2	1
Child-rearing practices are jointly agreed to.	1	2	3
My spouse and I support one another in disagreements with our children.	1	2	3
There are many big fights in our family.	3	2	1
My spouse and I do not handle family controversy well.	3	2	1
My spouse and I prevent our respective families from interfering in our lives.	1	2	3
I compete with other family members.	3	2	1
My spouse and I regularly discuss and plan how to handle our parents when they get older.	1	2	3
My total score			_____

Finances

	No	Sometimes	Yes
I manage my financial affairs well.	1	2	3
I have a lot of debts to worry about.	3	2	1
I have financial goals that I strive to achieve.	1	2	3
I have lost money through bad investments.	3	2	1
I plan my major purchases carefully.	1	2	3
I never have enough money.	3	2	1
My partner and I share common financial objectives.	1	2	3
I don't think about money or wealth.	3	2	1
I am ambitious and want to be financially successful.	1	2	3
I don't trust other people with my money.	3	2	1
I look for opportunities to earn more money.	1	2	3
I have not accumulated any money.	3	2	1
I invest my money for retirement.	1	2	3
I work hard but am not paid accordingly.	3	2	1
I enjoy what money can buy.	1	2	3
My total score			_____

Health

	No	Sometimes	Yes
I feel energetic and full of life.	1	2	3
I smoke.	3	2	1
I fall asleep easily and stay asleep.	1	2	3
I am tense and uptight.	3	2	1
I have few aches and pains.	1	2	3
I get more than an average number of colds and flus.	3	2	1
I have a good appetite and eat well.	1	2	3
I have a lot of headaches.	3	2	1
I try to stay fit by exercising at least three times a week.	1	2	3
I am overweight.	3	2	1
I get "down" a lot.	3	2	1
I drink alcohol to excess.	3	2	1
I am able to relax and take it easy.	1	2	3
I eat too many high-fat or high-cholesterol foods.	3	2	1
I am out of breath a lot.	3	2	1
My total score			_____

Community

	No	Sometimes	Yes
I feel part of my community.	1	2	3
I don't trust my neighbors.	3	2	1
I get involved in community activities.	1	2	3
I isolate myself from others.	3	2	1
I have a lot of neighbors and am known for being helpful.	1	2	3
I rarely speak with my neighbors.	3	2	1
I know our local politician and he or she knows me.	1	2	3
Neighbors don't even know I exist.	3	2	1
I help organize the annual street party.	1	2	3
I quarrel with my neighbors.	3	2	1
I keep a watch over my neighbor's house, especially when they are on vacation.	1	2	3
I can't be bothered socializing with neighbors.	3	2	1
My neighbors and I look after one another.	1	2	3
I don't like my neighbors knowing my business.	3	2	1
I am friendly with the neighborhood kids.	1	2	3
My total score			_____

References

Bandura, A. (1986). *Social foundations of thought and action: A social cognitive theory*. Englewood Cliffs, NJ: Prentice-Hall.

Beck, A.T. (1999).*The cognitive basis of anger, hostility and violence*. New York: Harper Collins.

Beck, A.T., Emery, G., & Greenberg, R.L. (2005). *Anxiety disorders and phobias*. Cambridge, MA: Basic Books.

Beck, J.S. (2005). *Cognitive therapy for challenging problems*. New York: Guilford Press.

Borysenko, J. (1987). *Minding the body, mending the mind*. Reading, MA: Addison-Wesley.

Burns, D.D. (2006). *The new drug-free anxiety therapy that can change your life*. New York: Morgan Road Books.

Clark, D.A., & Beck, A.T. (1999). *Scientific foundations of cognitive theory and therapy for depression*. New York: John Wiley and Sons.

Cousins, N. (1981). *Anatomy of an illness*. New York: Bantam.

De Bono, E. (1984). *Tactics: The art and science of success*. Boston: Little Brown.

Economic Business Roundtable (2006). Reducing the social and economic burden of mental disabilities in the workplace. Global Business and Economic Roundtable on Addiction and Mental Health, Canada.

Ellis, A. (1985). *Overcoming resistance: Rational emotive therapy with difficult clients*. New York: Springer.

Ellis, A. (1996). *Better, deeper, and more enduring brief therapy: The rational emotive behavior therapy approach.* New York: Brunner Mazel.

Ellis, A. (2000). *Feeling better, getting better, and staying better.* Atascadero, CA: Impact Publishers.

Ellis, A. (2000). *How to control your anxiety before it controls you.* New York: Citadel Press.

Ellis, A. (2001). *Overcoming destructive beliefs, feelings, and behaviors.* Amherst, NY: Prometheus Books.

Ellis, A. (2002). *Overcoming resistance: A rational emotive behavior therapy integrative approach.* New York: Springer.

Ellis, A. (2003). *Anger: How to live with and without it.* New York: Citadel Press.

Ellis, A. (2004). *Rational emotive behavior therapy it works for me—It can work for you.* Amherst, NY: Prometheus Books.

Ellis, A. (2004). *The road to tolerance: The philosophy of rational emotive behavior therapy.* Amherst, NY: Prometheus Books.

Ellis, A. (2006). *How to stubbornly refuse to make yourself miserable about anything—Yes anything.* New York: Citadel Press.

Ellis, A., & Becker, I. (1982). *A guide to personal happiness.* North Hollywood, California: Wilshire Books.

Ellis, A., & Bernard, M.E. (Eds.). (1985). *Clinical applications of rational-emotive therapy.* New York: Plenum.

Ellis, A., & Harper, R. (1975). *A new guide to rational living.* North Hollywood, CA: Wilshire Books.

EthicScan Ltd. (2005). Corporate ethics monitor, Canada.

Friedman, M., & Rosenman, R.H. (1974). *Type A behavior and your heart.* New York: Knopf.

Freudenberger, H.J., & Richelson, G. (1981). *Burnout: How to beat the high cost of success.* New York: Bantam.

Goldberg, L., & Breznitz, S. (Eds.). (1982). *Handbook of stress: Theoretical and clinical aspects.* New York: Free Press.

Klarreich, S. (Ed.). (1987). *Health and fitness in the workplace: Health education in business organizations.* New York: Praeger Press.

Klarreich, S. (1990). *Work without stress.* New York: Brunner Mazel.

Klarreich, S. (1992). *It can't happen to me: How to overcome 99 of life's most distressing problems.* New York: Brunner Mazel.

Klarreich, S. (Ed.). (1998). *Handbook of organizational health psychology: Programs to make the workplace healthier.* Madison, CT: Psychosocial Press.

Klarreich, S., Francek, J.L., & Moore, C.E. (Eds.). (1985). *The human resources management handbook: Principles and practice of employee assistance programs.* New York: Praeger.

Knaus, W. J. (1994). *Change your life now: Powerful techniques for positive change.* New York: Wiley.

Lange, A.J., & Jakubowski, P. (1976). *Responsible assertive behavior.* Champaign, IL: Research Press.

Lazarus, R.S. (1991). *Emotion and adaptation.* New York: Oxford.

Lazarus, R.S., & Folkman, S. (1984). *Stress, appraisal and coping.* New York: Springer.

Meichenbaum, D., & Jaremko, M.E. (Eds.). (1983). *Stress reduction and prevention.* New York: Plenum.

Machlowitz, M. (1980). *Workaholics: Living with them, working with them.* Reading, MA: Addison-Wesley.

Pelletier, K.R. (1984). *Healthy people in unhealthy places.* Monterey, CA: Merloyd, Lawrence.

Pines, A., & Aronson, E. (1981). *Burnout: From tedium to personal growth.* New York: Free Press.

Seligman, M.F.P. (2002). *Authentic happiness.* New York: Free Press.

Snyder, C.R. & Shane, J.L. (Eds.). (2002). *Handbook of positive psychology.* New York: Oxford University Press

Watson Wyatt Survey (2005). Staying at work, Canada.

Index

A

Y